Something Worth Reading for Inspiration

Haripada Dhar

To order additional copies of this book, contact:
Xlibris
1-888-795-4274
www.Xlibris.com
Orders@Xlibris.com
761746

Contents

I prayed to the Lord that I could pass on the collected information in the form of a book to the future and younger generations. I dedicate this book to the younger generation and to all wishing to improve themselves. God Bless You All!

HARIPADA DHAR
May 2017

PREFACE

About last fifteen years I have been collecting materials for possible putting them together in the form of a presentation. Our temple in the College Station Area in Texas, USA has been in existence about that many years for regular weekend gathering. The temple brought along opportunities for presentations and enthusiasms among participants of different age groups. I was one of the persons making frequent presentations to the temple audience. My presentations were well-received by those attending the temple functions. People would come forward and expressed their satisfaction −nice talk; I liked your speech, etc.

I was a Post-Doctoral Fellow of Professor John Bockris in his laboratory at the Texas A&M University. He made congratulatory remarks when I was in his group and also when I was working in my own company, BCS Fuel Cells, Inc.

Any type of concentration that is required for any vocation, activities or profession can be considered meditation. This is a rather broader definition of meditation. Only thing lacking may be physical exercises of some kind. Dr. Bockris used to concentrate on a fixed spot on the wall. His group was well aware of his practicing meditation this way. Dr. Bockris showed his capability benefiting immensely from meditation. My liking of meditation led me thinking of these techniques of topics of meditation and philosophical discussions of Maya and *Avidya* (cosmic and individual delusions) and led me to the discussions of these topics in Gita.

Meditation is important and beneficial; one would think everyone would show interest and start practicing it. But this is not what is generally observed. There is hardly any interest in most people, let alone the younger people who would get most benefit out of meditation. There are two groups of reasons that people are not inclined to meditation.

In this world and the society, God has placed each of us in particular places and circumstances. We according to our own action (karma), evolution, education, talents and abilities earn our living. Can everyone become rich? It may or may not be possible. But can everyone improve their lot they are in and become successful and/or happier? The answer is firmly affirmative. If one meditates regularly, one can achieve this modest goal.

People do not habitually learn meditation because they are not exposed to it from their childhood. Another group of reasons includes forces of opposition in our minds discussed in Chapter 1 of Bhagavad Gita. Everyday battle involves (1) self-control versus self-indulgence; (2) discriminative intelligence versus mental resistance; (3) spiritual resolve in meditation versus mental resistance and physical restlessness; and (4) soul-consciousness versus ignorance and attraction to lower ego nature.

Most people ignore meditation because of the presence of forces of opposition in our minds and in our nature. These forces of opposition have been discussed in Chapter 1 of Bhagavad Gita. It is hard to give up sense pleasures for unknown happiness that may come in the future with regular practice of meditation. These are the reasons people would rather live a life they are used to rather than learn techniques of meditation, and lead a better life.

God does not reward or punish anyone. He has given us the power to reward or punish us by the use of our own reason and will-power. We should strengthen our minds and refuse to carry on the burden of mental and moral weaknesses acquired in the past years, and burn them in the fires of the present resolution and right activities.

We are all parts of the divine. Our life sparks—our souls come from God. We are spiritual beings. We have the divine heritage. Upon taking birth we come in contact with what is called material contamination. Under influence of God's energy of Maya, we forget, ignore, or disregard our divine roots. Thus we start our lives in this physical world. Every stage of spiritual development is achieved by the Grace of God, blessings of the guru and by the disciple's loyal practice of guru's teachings. Everything comes in time. The goal is not to leave the body, but rather live in tune with God and immersed in His love.

How hard you have to try to get something you really want to have? *Babaji advises until you can tire patience with patience.* Babaji waited 48 days outside the ashram (hermitage) of Agastyar to receive initiation into kriya yoga. Then 18 long months he spent learning of yogic disciplines. Babaji obtained a state of Soruba Samadhi wherein divinity descended, transformed the causal, subtle and physical bodies. The physical bodies cease to age (what is Soruba Samadhi).

In one talk I wanted to clarify the differences between nine planets (*navagrahas*) in the *Vedic* tradition and modern scientific tradition (of the solar system). Nine planets in the solar system are Mercury, Venus, Earth, Mars, Jupiter, Saturn, Uranus, Neptune, and Pluto. Whereas, nine planets in the Vedic tradition are as follows: Sun, Mercury, Venus, Moon, Rahu, Ketu, Mars, Jupiter, and Pluto.

Where is Lord Krishna?
How can we find Him?

Lord Krishna is worshipped as the 8th incarnation of Lord Vishnu, the supreme Lord representing the preservation aspect of the whole creation. The word "Krishna" means black, which represents mysteriousness. Krishna's body color is blue—young rain-laden cloud color with a bluish tinge. Lord Krishna holds and plays a flute. The music of the flute creates "breeze" or spiritual energy that a devotee may feel in various forms running through the body. The sensation could be feeling heat or cold, or a feeling of peace and bliss through the body and the spine. The flute represents the *shushumna*, the center of the astral spine in the body (equivalent to the spinal cord in the physical body). The holes of the flutes represent the seven *chakras* in the astral body (see Introduction to Meditation and the Chakras). The *chakras* are the centers of human evolution. So, the playing of the flute by Lord Krishna means: He is the sole doer in our body guiding us higher and higher in our evolutionary process.

I would like to explore how we can connect to Lord Krishna in our present incarnation. Where is Lord Krishna?

In Gita verse 7.7, the Lord proclaims
matta parataram nanyat kinchitasti dhananjay
mayi sarvamidam protam sutre maniganaiva

Translation: There is nothing higher than Me. Everything is strung on Me like clusters of gems on a string. Lord Krishna is our supreme God.

1

In Gita verse 18.61, the Lord proclaims
iswara sarvabhutanam hriddeshe arjuna tisthati
bhramayan sarvabhutani yantrarudhani mayaa

Translation: God is residing in the hearts of all beings. He causes all beings to revolve by His power of Maya, as if they are mounted on a machine.

Lord is omnipresent, but His special place is the heart of all beings. Compelled by the power of the God's law of Maya the delusive force, all beings are veritably bound by its working principles. God is hidden behind the veils of Maya. Man has to work hard to remove the veils and find the omnipresent God.

The Lord is so close to us. Why can't we find Him? Let us consider an analogy: this world in the form a party given by the Lord. If someone gives a party, and no one comes, what kind of a party would that be? Or, will you give a party, if you knew no one is coming? There would be no party at all! The creator created this earth and the universe with its innumerable galaxies and stars, and all the imaginable or unimaginable aspects associated with the creation.

Our habitat, this earth, is wonderful in all respects, extraordinarily created and teeming with all kinds of living beings; humans are at the top of the creation. Our growth potential is practically unlimited as each one of us in essence is pure consciousness, which is also the essence of God. God is *satchidananda*—consciousness, existence, and bliss.

The Lord made this universe for us to inhabit and enjoy.

Also, importantly, if a party is given, the guests come, and the guests do not see the hosts. What kind of a party would that be?

We came here. But where is the Creator? We do not see Him. He is hiding behind His creation casting a spell of illusion on us. He also wanted us to find Him. This is the aim of our life to find God, the Creator.

We have come to Lord Krishna's party. We must try to find Him while we are here in this lifetime. Our life—this body temple is very unique, rare, and precious for engaging in the search of the Lord. At the same time, our time is very short. We must go for this opportunity very fast.

The Lord hides from His creation by casting nets of illusions. There are two modes of illusions: Maya and *Avidya*. The vehicles of Maya are the triple qualities: *satta*, *rajas*, and *tamas*. People generally cannot escape anyone of these qualities. You may be very good in every way, that is, you have predominantly *satta* quality, but you are still under the influence of Maya. These triple qualities are the vehicles of Maya or the carrier of the Lord's energy of Maya: the cosmic delusion.

Through the power of Maya, God creates, sustains, and dissolves the worlds and beings.

The state of the influence of *Maya* on us can be compared to that of being under hypnotism. The hypnotized person cannot get out of his unreal state without being de-hypnotized. To be able to remove this spell of Maya and see God, one has to surrender to the Lord. In Gita verse 7.14,

Lord declares:
daivi hi-easha gunamayi mama maya duratyaa
mameva yo prapadyante mayametam taranti-te

Translation: This divine Maya of mine is composed of the triple qualities is difficult to cross over, but those who surrender to Me, they alone are able to cross over.

Once de-hypnotized, the person can then return to the perception of the pure soul and united to the Spirit—Lord Krishna. How do we surrender?

Lord declares in Gita verse 18.65
manmana bhava madbhakta madyaji mam namaskuru
mameva aeshyashi satyam te pratijane priyaoshi me

Translation: Fix your mind on Me, be devoted to Me, sacrifice to Me, offer adorations to Me, you will indeed attain Me. This truly I promise to you, because you are My very dear friend.

A person should strive to get company of good people, follow virtuous ways and guidance of a Master, and most importantly, practice meditation, that is, yoga as mentioned in the Gita. Through the cumulative effects of meditation, he should remain ever calm and spiritually watchful. These are the practical methods to neutralize the effects of delusion. *Paramahamsa Yogananda* emphasized meditation being the quickest method for spiritual advancement.

The other illusion net is the casting of a personality (or individuality) to each of us. This is known as *Avidya*. Everyone builds his/her own world under the spell of these two nets of illusions. God's Mayic power of creation is inherited by everyone in the form of *Avidya*—each one of us is a mini creator fashioning good or evil for himself and the world of which he is a part. The influence of the force of this *Avidya* is such that no matter how strong is the illusion, man does not want to part with it.

Maya and *Avidya*—universal and individual delusion—give man a body and a mind with which to play a part in the cosmic drama of the Lord's creation. *Avidya*, the second net of illusion, cast on man, has some uses in this world. It leads to worldly success, which is a requirement for being born in this world. Our primary objective is to be one with the Lord at the same time to engage ourselves fruitfully to the services of others.

Too much *Avidya* leads to extreme materialism. A balance needs to be achieved between Avidya and the real knowledge for shaking the illusion of mini-creatorship and understanding that the real dower is the Lord Himself: I am just an instrument in His hands.

With balanced living of culturing spirituality and worldly engagements, the cosmic delusion of Maya and the individual delusion of *Avidya* will weaken, and a picture will gradually emerge as the Lord being the sole existence that exists.

Sage, mystic and philosopher Swami *Omkarananda Saraswati* (who initiated me to a *japa mantra* for which I am very grateful), a direct disciple of Swami Sivananda of Rishikesh (India), describes *Avidya* as follows: 'Ignorance (*Avidya*) is a powerful magician in the human mind. It makes invisible that which is most visible—God.'

The goal of life is to find God. Lord Krishna is our Supreme God. Lord is saying that I invited you, and you came. However you will not see me automatically. In order for us to find the Lord, we have to follow the teachings of the Gita verse 18.65, mentioned earlier. The goal of life is to be God realized. As I am making my small efforts in that direction, naturally questions arise as to how to be God realized? Today's talk makes an effort to understand Lord Krishna and His presence in our lives. This talk is as important to me as it should be to you.

Prayer:

O Lord, thank you for this opportunity for us to be together here (temple at Navasota, Texas, USA) on the occasion of *Janmastami* (Birth ceremony of Lord Krishna). We have been blessed by the remembrance of your holy name. O Lord, help us and guide us so that we can engage ourselves in spiritual activities and see through the forces of Maya and *Avidya* your presence in our lives and everywhere. Thank you, thank you, and thank you.

Lord Krishna's Supreme Personality according to Bhagavad-Gita

om kasturitilakam lalatapatale bakshasthale kaustabham
nasagre baramauktikam kartale benum kare kankanam
sarbaange harichandam sulalitam kanthe cha muktabalim
gopastri paribestitham gopala churamanim

Translation: Salutation to Lord Krishna! Think of the Lord surrounded by the loving milkmaids of Vrindaban. He is wearing a tilak mark of kasturi musk on His broad forehead, a *kaustabha* jewel on His chest, a big jewel in between His eyebrows. His hands adorned with bracelets holding the flute. His whole body has fragrance of sandal wood perfume. A pearl necklace adorns around sweet-voiced His neck. The crest jewel, named Gopala, on the crown shines on His head.

What does supreme personality mean? How do we know Lord Krishna is the Supreme God? What did He reveal in the Gita about His being the Supreme Personality?

Our essence is spiritual. We are not fully happy – our search for happiness does not end until our awareness is restored to God's wholeness.

The quickest way for human beings to achieve the experience of the Supreme Truth is to have a form, a name, and a personality of God. This God can be Lord Krishna, the Divine Mother, Shiva, Jesus Christ, or the personal *Ishtha Devata* (personal favorite God).

We know Lord Krishna is the son of Devaki and Vasudeva, brought up by Yosoda and Nanda.

In Gita verse 8.8 Lord Krishna mentions He is the *"param purusham"* – Effulgent Self – the Supreme *Purusha* (Lord Himself).

In verses 7.21, 7.22, and 7.23, Lord Krishna tells: Whatever divine form the devotee wishes to worship, in that very form I intensify his faith.

It is I who bestow upon him the fulfillment of his desires. The worshippers of Gods go to the Gods, while those who are my devotee come to me.

I would like to explore from the verses of Bhagavad-Gita, what Lord Krishna has revealed about His being the Supreme God. Here is a short summary of few essential verses.

The existence of God is immanent and also transcendent. Immanence relates to the physical world – whatever we can see with our eyes and mind can feel. Transcendence relates to that existing beyond the physical world – worlds and realms that we cannot see, but surely exist.

In Gita verse 9.4, Lord Krishna says, the entire universe is pervaded by Me in My un-manifested form, all beings exist in me, but I do not abide in them. Lord Krishna further says in verse 9.6 that just as the mighty wind that moves everywhere abides in the sky, in the same way all beings abide in me.

A small example of immanence and transcendence follows: Water can exist in an invisible form in the form of vapor. The unseen water vapor can be condensed into liquid water and then frozen into ice. So, the invisible and impersonal God can be projected into a form and worshipped as a personality. However, a devotee should not alone associate God to that form, and forgets His omnipresence. Sri Ramakrishna, who saw God constantly as Mother Kali, later said: "I had to destroy that finite form of my Mother with the sword of wisdom, to behold her as the formless infinite." He who worships God merely as the finite form will not attain the transcendental divine union with His infinite nature.

In verse 8.21, the Lord says, the Un-manifest Being is called the Imperishable, which the scriptures declare as the Supreme Goal. That is My highest abode reaching which, one does not return to this physical world again.

Lord Krishna tells in verse 12.5, those who worship the non-manifest absolute have to encounter greater difficulties because it is very difficult for an embodied soul to reach the non-manifest absolute. A form of the Divine is better for worshipping.

In Gita verse 7.7 the Lord says, there is nothing higher than Me. Everything is strung on me like clusters of gems on a string.

In verse 4.11, the Lord says, however a person worships (adores) Me, in the same manner I bestow My grace on him. All human beings follow My path various ways.

In verse 9.22, the Lord assures, those who worship Me by meditating upon Me with a vision of non-separateness and who are ceaselessly devoted to Me, I look after what they have and give what they need.

In verse 9.23, the Lord declares that even the devotees of other Gods who practice devotion with faith are in fact worshipping Me alone but doing so indirectly. The apparent polytheism, many perceive Hinduism is, is in fact monotheism.

In verse 8.9, the Lord says, He is the omniscient, the ancient, the ruler of all, the subtler than the subtlest, the supporter of all, of the form inconceivable, effulgent like the sun, and beyond darkness.

In verse 9.18, the Lord says, I am the Final Goal, the Nourisher of all beings, the Lord of creation, the Witnessing Self, the Supreme Abode, the Refugee of all, the Supreme Well-wisher. I am the origin and dissolution of the universe; I am also the sustainer, the supreme treasure, and the imperishable seed.

In verse 7.10, the Lord says, Know Me to be the eternal seed of all beings. I am the intellect in the wise, the valor of those who are valiant.

In verse 14.27, the Lord says, I am the basis of the Absolute *Brahman* (the Infinite), the Immortal, the Indestructible, and of Eternal virtue, and unending Bliss.

In verse 14.4, the Lord says, whatever embodied being is born in any species (according their past deeds) it is I who am the seed (Divine Intelligence) giving Father while *Prakriti* (Mother Nature) is the conceiving mother.

In verse 15.7, the Lord says, in this world of embodied beings a ray of My eternal Self exists as the individual soul, attracts to itself five senses and the mind.

Arjuna, who treated Krishna as his friend and charioteer, was fortunate to observe the Lord's universal form, and declares in verse 11.18, You are the Imperishable Brahman, the Supreme Knowable. You are the best Support of the Universe, the Imperishable Protector of the Eternal Religion. Further in 11.42, Arjuna pleads: out of mere fun and play, whatever disrespect I have shown you, while sleeping, sitting, and taking food, in privacy or before others, I pray, O Invincible and Boundless One, for your forgiveness.

The Lord says in verses 12.6 and 12.7, those who have offered all actions to Me, meditate upon Me with one-pointed mind, whose minds are immersed in Me, I become their savior in a very short time.

In summary, the Lord says in verses 18.61 and 18.62

isvarah sarva-bhutanam hrddese arjuna tissthati
bhramayan sava-bhutani yantrarudhani mayaya.

tam eva saranam gaccha sarva-bhavena bharata
tat-prasadat param santim sthanam prapsyasi sasvata

Translation: The Lord is situated in everyone's heart. By His power of cosmic delusion (Maya) compels all beings to rotate as if attached to a machine. O Arjuna take refuge in Him alone with all your being. By His grace, you will attain supreme peace and supreme abode.

Lord Krishna is the Supreme God.

Maya & *Avidya*
(Delusions—Cosmic & Individual)

Delusion has two parts: Cosmic or Universal delusion (Maya) and individual delusion (*Avidya*). Maya and *Avidya* give man a body and a mind with which to play a part in the cosmic drama of the Lord's creation. The concepts of Maya and *Avidya* are intimately related. Maya refers to the Creator (God) and *Avidya* to an individual.

God evolves soul out of Him and hypnotizes them by delusion perceiving themselves into human or animal bodies. This is cosmic delusion of multiplicity. God is behind the creation, but no one really realizes that He is behind the creation. Under the influence of Maya, the soul becomes a limited ego, which identifies itself with the body, and the body's relatives and possessions, thus comes under the influence of *Avidya*. Once so identified, soul can no longer express its omnipresence, omniscience, and omnipotence. This is similar to the situation of a rich prince in a state of amnesia wandering in slums might imagine himself to be a pauper.

Avidya is the individual cosmic hypnosis or illusion. It is imposed on all beings. *Avidya* makes them express, perceive, and interact with one another as though each has its own separate reality. God creates through the power of Maya. Man has inherited God's Mayic power of creation in the form of *Avidya*. Through the instruments of mind, intelligence, and sensory organs of perception and action, man creates his own illusion of reality. Thus, he is a miniature creator fashioning good or evil for him and the world of which he is a part. It is the creative force inherent in man's thoughts that make him so formidable. The influence of the force of *Avidya* is such that no matter how strong the illusion, man does not want to part with it. He is very much opinionated; and therein is the ignorance. He perceives the temporal world as the reality, eternal substance—in so far he is able to grasp the concept of eternity. He imagines the grossness of sensory experience to be pure essence of feeling and perception. He fabricates his own standard of morality and behavior.

However, nothing can exist without the principle of individuality. If *Avidya* were completely withdrawn, the form that it maintains would re-dissolve into the formless Spirit.

Avidya leads to some worldly success, which is a requirement for being born in the world. Our primary objective for being here on the earth is liberation of consciousness to the wholeness of God and at the same time to engage ourselves fruitfully to the service of others to achieve the needed worldly success.

Too much *Avidya* leads to extreme materialism, for which the West has been accused of. Eastern countries, in general, are thought to be more spiritually inclined and people in general have less of *Avidya*. A balance needs to be achieved between *Avidya* and the real knowledge (spiritual) for shaking the illusion of mini-creatorship and understanding the real dower is the Lord Himself: I am just an instrument in His hands.

On the other hand, much opinionated views on a particular idea, mode of living, or faith can lead to extremism, which can be harmful, and can impede success and progress. One can be opinionated and at the same time be open to the possibility of better alternative elsewhere. Extremism in one form or other is seen everywhere on this earth. It can be individuals, group of people, society, or in a country. The reason behind any spirituality is to understand who we are and what the nature of God is.

The sentient beings are far removed from their perfect Essence. Why do beings not know they are Spirit and behave accordingly? God's will to create is the original cause. God's creative power is *Shakti* or *Maha Prakriti*. The conglomerate workings of the principles of God's creation are collectively called Maya, or the cosmic delusion. God and His Cosmic Nature in the microcosmic form are present in the human body as the pure soul and pure human nature. The pure soul and the pure human nature become distorted into the human ego and sentient human nature, owing to the temporary identification of the perfect soul with the imperfect body. This is the working principle of Maya.

Maya is a cosmic hypnosis that veils the Singular Reality and imposes the suggestions of manifestation. The cosmic consciousness of One Perceiver (God), experiencing these transformations of *Maya*, becomes correspondingly individualized as many souls. The soul, experiencing and interacting with the workings and manifestations of cosmic delusion

Maya, has his own identity, *Avidya*, the individual delusion, and thereby becomes the body-identified ego. Like the Spirit, the soul is ever pure and unchanged. Attuned to the divine intelligence of the indwelling soul, the resultant being is pure, noble, and wise. But the more the consciousness yields to the worldly processes through the sensory mind, the more limited and deluded the ego becomes. But even if it sinks to the depths of ignorance and evil, the consciousness never loses its divine soul potential.

A hypnotist may suggest to a subject that he sees a tiger. The subject sees the tiger and cries in terror. The hypnotist only suggested the vision of the tiger, but did not ask the subject to be afraid of it. God the Master Hypnotist, through His power of Maya has suggested to individualized souls to visualize the universe with all its intricacies and details. The perceptions of the individualized consciousness, being personalized by *Avidya* (individual delusion), become elaborated by feeling. Under the influence of the sensory mind, feeling expresses itself as emotions—such as fear, attachment, repulsion, desire, etc. The Master Hypnotist did not suggest that individualized souls should be afraid or courageous, miserable or happy. These are their personal creations.

Maya does not affect God, in the same way that poison does not affect the snake. To remedy the situation of the clutch of *Maya*, the intelligent man should remain in good company; or at least, should remove himself from the evil company. Poisoned from birth by Maya, he should strive to meet good persons, follow virtuous ways and the guidance of a true guru, and, most importantly practice yoga (meditation) learning from a Master. Through the cumulative effects of meditation, he should remain ever calm and spiritually watchful. These are practical methods to neutralize the effects of delusion, Maya and *Avidya.*

With a balanced living the cosmic delusion of Maya and individual delusion of *Avidya* will weaken and picture will gradually immerge as the Lord being the sole existence in everything that exists.

The real reason for being in the world is to awaken from the conditioned states of our mind and consciousness to Self and God realizations. It is a very gradual process to come out from this conditioned states. Human being has a free will: he can choose what he wants to do or not to do. At the start, acknowledge that we are immortal spiritual beings expressing through our minds and the physical bodies. As an individualized unit of the supreme Reality, we can know it as it is and know our true nature by choosing to rise above ordinary states of mind and consciousness.

The Creator created this beautiful earth, the universe with its innumerable galaxies and stars, and all the imaginable and unimaginable aspects associated with the creation. He has made this for us to inhabit and enjoy. He wanted us to come. The party was given for us indeed! We have come to the party given by the Lord, but we do not see Him. He is hiding behind His creation. He also wanted us to find Him. This is the aim of our life: to find God, the Creator. We have to find Him while we are here on earth in this lifetime.

The Lord hides from His creation by casting nets of illusions. He brings every one under one of the three modes of qualities: *sattwa, rajas,* and *tamas.* People generally cannot escape any one of these qualities. You may be very good in every way, that is, you have predominantly *sattwa* quality, but you are under the influence of Maya. The triple qualities are the vehicle of Maya or the carrier of the Lord's energy of Maya: the cosmic delusion. The other illusion net is the casting of a personality (individuality) to each of us or *Avidya*, as mentioned earlier. Everyone builds his/her own world under the spell of these two nets of illusions.

Under the spell of Maya, one could be good, passionate (active), or evil. Any of these triple qualities brings one under the spell of Maya.

This is a kind of state comparable to be under hypnotism. The hypnotized person cannot get out of his unreal state without being de-hypnotized. To be able to remove the spell of Maya, one has to surrender to the Lord.

By wisdom and self-analysis and by the Grace of God, man can get himself de-hypnotized from Maya and the individual delusion, *Avidya*. He can then return to the perception of the pure soul and united to the Spirit.

If we are attuned to the indwelling soul, we are pure, noble, and wise. But the more we yield to the worldly processes through the sensory mind, the more limited and deluded our ego becomes. But even if our consciousness sinks to the depths of ignorance and evil, the consciousness never loses its divine soul potential.

Through the power of Maya, God creates, sustains, and dissolves the worlds and beings.

Maya is the phenomenal world of separate objects and people, which creates for many the illusion that it is the only reality. For mystics this manifestation is real, but it is a fleeting reality. It is a mistake to believe Maya represents a fundamental reality. Each person, each object, from the perspective of eternity is like a brief, disturbed drop of water from an unbounded ocean.

The goal of enlightenment is to understand this or to experience this—to see intuitively that the distinction between the Self and the Universe is a false dichotomy (division into two parts).

Maya must be seen through to achieve moksha (liberation)—*ahamkara* (egoism) and *karma* (action) are seen as part of the binding forces of *Maya.*

Maya is neither true nor untrue. Since *Brahman* (the Absolute without any attributes) is the only truth, Maya cannot be true. Since Maya causes the material world to be seen, it cannot be untrue. Hence Maya is indescribable.

Maya has two principal functions:

- Cover up *Brahman* and hide from our mind.
- Present the material world instead of *Brahman*.

Unenlightened *jivas* (living beings) are the servants of Maya, hence they are in misery.

With a balanced living Maya and *Avidya* will weaken and a picture will gradually immerge as the Lord being the sole existence in everything that exists.

Japa and Meditation

Japa is concentrating on a mantra, usually mantra based on a God's name. *Japa* is very helpful for achieving mind control. Techniques of japa are used sometimes before meditation for achieving internalization. Meditation can then proceed. In the meditation routine, we use the techniques of conscious breathing to achieve internalization. The technique of Mantra repetition (*japa*) can be also used to achieve the same.

Japa not only helps to control the mind, it also develops love for God. *Japa* has various levels of achievements. For example, the mental *japa* is more effective in producing calmness, reducing stress, making health better, etc. all these benefits are there for doing the japa.

Japa is a form of meditation, but it is not the actual meditation process in the way that meditation is practiced.

Meditation is a much more rapid process for developing spirituality. The worldly benefits are more quickly achieved.

I would like to suggest that the students of meditation also practice *japa*, at least one round of the *japa* bead. One round constitutes repeating 108 times of the *japa mantra*. It need not be at the same time of meditation; can be any other time.

Those who do not practice meditation should at least practice *japa*. Those who practice meditation should practice also *japa* to get the most benefit out of both. *Japa* helps the meditation practice leading to more thoughtless and deeper states. These benefits are both worldly and spiritual.

Meditation—What it is and its Benefits

Meditation is internalization of the mind. It is a process of mind control. Mind is our faculty for thinking. In Gita verse 7.4 the Lord says: My manifested nature has eight-fold differentiation—earth, water, fire, air, ether (sky), mind, intellect, and false ego (I am, It is mine). Mind and intellect form the essence of human personality, and constitute part of the subtle body. The subtle body survives the death of the physical body. It is for our overall wellbeing that mind control is necessary through meditation and concentration.

Our physical conditions can influence our minds. If the mind is controlled, our physical conditions and body functions improve. One of the most widely perceived benefits of mind control is Stress Control. If you meditate, you will overcome your stress problems. One of the extremes of mind control could be a miracle. Our mind has the capability for accomplishing miracles. Mind produces thoughts. Thoughts are form of aids for accomplishing what is desired. If our thoughts are strong enough, which comes from a controlled mind, and then thoughts can be materialized. Power of the mind can be compared with the sun's rays. Sun's rays can be converged with the help of mirror and used to generate fire. In the same way our thoughts can be converted to be more effective and powerful.

If you meditate, your parents and relatives will feel happy about you. They will know that you can take care of yourself under various conditions of your life. In the same way, if you have dependents, who meditate, you will feel less anxious about them; feel more secure about them knowing that your dependents can take care of themselves.

Arjuna says in Gita verses 6.33-34, it is difficult to control the mind than it is difficult to control the wind. Lord Krishna says in verse 6.35, in fact it is difficult, but it can be controlled with repeated practice of meditation.

If you learn the techniques of meditation, then at any time you are troubled, in bad situation, in worries, you can take shelter in your inside; and consciously become worry-free.

Benefits of Meditation

- Controls stress and strain of daily work routine
- Refines and rejuvenates the nervous system
- Slows down the biological aging process
- Increase the immune strength
- Grows the capability of doing many things at the same time.
- Grows calmness and quietness—but a dynamo in doing work
- Goes above pettiness
- Improves functions of all glands and internal organs
- Restore hormonal imbalances
- Can help certain problems dealing with birth conceptions—has been mentioned by *Paramahamsa Hariharananda* in his book on Kriya Yoga
- Positive thinking develops. Overall health improves. Appreciation for living increases. Evolutionary progress occurs

Meditation—Introduction to Meditation and Chakras

Our spine is most important in our bodies for our evolution. There are three bodies: physical, astral or subtle (body of light), and causal (ideational). Along the spine in the subtle body, there are seven subtle energy centers, known as chakras. These centers are from the bottom of spine: *Muladhar, Swadhistan, Manipur, Anahata, Visuddha, Ajna, and Sahasrara.* During meditation, we can access our subtle bodies and nourish them. A discussion of different positions of chakras and their functions when they are developed through meditation constitutes an introduction to meditation, or Chakra Meditation.

An example of building a home is considered here to have little more understanding of the three bodies. Causal: means reason for everything, ideas for everything. You have your idea of the design. Subtle: you make the design in the paper and maybe build a prototype small home.

Physical: you build the home. When you destroy the home, you have only destroyed the physical home. But the subtle and the causal homes survive. In time, of course, you can also destroy the subtle and the causal.

In the subtle realm, there is no time factor. That is why when you meditate deeply, time passes quickly; you have no sense of time. All thinking is done in the subtle realm.

Soul enters the fertilized egg wearing the subtle and causal bodies. The causal body is encased in the subtle body. The causal body is the cause of the other two bodies: physical and subtle. The creative faculty that we have is subtle and causal in nature. These two bodies build, maintain, and enliven the gross physical body. These two bodies (subtle and causal) are considered the instrumental of the soul. Our life, our ability to perceive through the senses and understand through our consciousness is dependent on the subtle powers and forces of the subtle and causal bodies.

Physical body is very limited. The subtle body is much bigger than the physical body. It contains the mind. The causal body is much bigger than the subtle body. Just like our body, there are also three universes: physical, subtle, and causal.

The creator made the causal body or the ideational body first, then subtle body of light, and then the physical body. Every day we are in our subtle and causal bodies unconsciously during sleep and deep sleeps so that our physical bodies can rest and vitalize and become ready for activities the following day.

Chakra means wheel – wheel of evolution. Each chakra is a psychic center. These chakras represent different levels of consciousness, the stages through which a soul passes on its journey towards perfection. Our various inherent qualities, and our innate nature are the reflection to the extent our chakras are developed.

The chakras are naturally developed to some extent in all of us. Further development of the chakras, requires practices of meditation. As we meditate the chakras develop, and we expand our consciousness and understanding, and improve our various functions, qualities, and abilities.

All chakras are connected and are developed during meditation. In the basic techniques we meditate on one or two chakras; since the chakras are connected, all are developed at the same time.

In all professions or activities one does for living and pleasures, one needs concentration; and concentration is a form of meditation using the subtle body and the chakras. **Thus everyone is meditating in one way or another.** The creativity or productivity achieved by the person depends on his level of development in his expertise.

Muladhar Chakra

The first chakra is *Muladhar,* at the bottom of the spine. It means "the main foundation". It also means "the basic receptacle". This chakra represents the instinctive nature of the person. When one gets awakened through meditation, one's consciousness rises above the animalistic tendencies and habits.

When the center is active, there is the negative expression of increased sensitivity and insecurity, increased sexual urge, desire for satisfying relationship, etc. When one begins to meditate, then complimentary attributes or qualities are awakened, and gradually one overcomes the negative qualities.

Muladhar chakra is the 'black hole' into which the divine faculties, humane qualities and the godly awareness of life are sucked into. We live in sensual pleasures and live life as people have for generations. Since we are so caught up in the powerful attraction of this black hole, there is no escape. It is here that the wheel of life or the law of karma is experienced. The person is caught up in the wheel of life and death.

Muladhara chakra is also known as the Money Center, because it is associated with the material world. To acquire anything in the world we need money. *Muladhara* is the place of money. It does not necessarily mean currency or coins. It means the physical resources or buying capacity of a person.

If you meditate you develop qualities to increase your marketability through the development of the *Muladhara* chakra. If a person meditates, he will be more liked by a potential employer if he is looking for a job. Such qualities as calmness, steadiness, and confidence are reflected by his demeanor. If you meditate on one chakra, all chakras are developed, since all chakras are connected. In advanced meditation techniques, one meditates on all the chakras. That is of course more beneficial.

Muladhara takes up our most of the time, life, and energy. We spend majority of our waking moments earning money, paying off debts, enjoying the present, and saving for the future. Our existence is ruled by this center. The development of the *Muladhara* chakra enhances our material prosperity by strengthening our earning potential. Riches, fame, luxuries, power are all benefits of a highly developed *Muladhara* chakra.

A benefit may have a down side. While focusing on the *Muladhara* opens up the abundance of the universe and makes grateful recipients, mere prosperity or fame without adequate understanding of the purpose can be detrimental. Those who meditate constantly will gain steadiness of mind. Such people can handle the material benefits of the *Muladhara* without losing their balance.

Lord Ganesh is the presiding deity at the *Muladhara* chakra. Big ears, long nose, small and sharp eyes are indicative of the receptive attitude needed for the intake of valuable knowledge, long nose indicates importance of breath control, small and sharp eyes indicate keen observation. The seed syllable, which a yogi concentrates on, is *lam* at this chakra.

Two sense organs are regulated by this center: nose and anus. Controls of these sense organs develop with the development of this *Muladhar* chakra.

The traits associated with it are power, vitality, and physical energy. The subtle center is a four- petal lotus. It indicates the amount of physical energy available and one's will to live in the material reality. It is believed to be the center point of the nerves related to the production and maintenance of bones, flesh, skin, and hair.

Muladhar is represented by a fiery triangle. It indicates that the soul is now caught in the trap of the three active forces of nature, the triple qualities—'sattva', 'rajas', and 'tamas'.

Swadhisthana Chakra

The second chakra is known as *Swadhisthana* chakra on the spine in the subtle body about 3.8 cm above the *Muladhara* chakra. The word means a place where the mind is established for a long time. It also means the "home of the (lower) self".

This center is located behind the genitals. It is also known as the sex center or family center. Up to this point, the embodied soul acts on purely animal or instinctual urges, exhibiting gross habits. The second chakra directs our energy into sexuality and pleasure, and has a strong hold over our emotions and passions. There is a six-petal lotus in this subtle center. It also reflects the ability to connect with another human on a deeply physical and spiritual level, both giving and receiving. Traits associated with the second center are personal expression, sexuality, creativity, confidence and the ability to love. Physiologically, production and maintenance of semen, fat, urine, and water is controlled from this chakra.

The presiding deity of this center is mother Durga, an aspect of the divine mother in the form of Shakti or energy. Mother Durga as the divine mother symbolizes the creative (or reproductive) aspect in us and also is the nurturing influence on our growth and survival. Whenever we are nurtured and cared for, it is the divine mother taking care of us. The subtle sound produced at this center is *bam*.

Two sense organs ruled by this center are tongue (organ of taste) and genitals (organ of reproduction). Moderation in eating and sexual activity is encouraged. Regular practice of meditation would help us to control the activity of our sense organs through the development of our chakras.

All we really *want* is uninterrupted happiness, the unending bliss found inside. Meditation or concentration is the way to go within. The sooner we learn to stop seeking temporary pleasure in the world, and dwell in the permanent joy of the soul, the sooner we reach our goal.

Manipur Chakra

It is the third one from the bottom on the spinal canal in our subtle body. This chakra is located at the back of the navel. It is known as the navel center and also known as the food center since it is the region where our food is digested. *Manipura* means the jewel center. It is a ten-petal lotus. The presiding deity is the Sun and the subtle sound produced is *rang*. In the food center we derive our physical energy, beauty, luster and vitality. Food, which is directly affected by the sunlight, has a strong influence on the mind and our tranquility.

The type of food we eat, and in the manner in which we eat it influences the mind. Gita verse 15.14 (Chapter and Verse) Lord says that God Himself burns as the fire at the navel center. So what we eat is an offering to Him. By meditation and developing the *Manipur* chakra, we can enjoy the food we eat and its effect on us will be wholly beneficial.

Two sense organs controlled by this center are eyes and the feet. Two sense organs are most used and abused. Through meditation, we learn to see the beauty everywhere in God's creation, and in the people around us.

The sensory organ, the feet, lead us into many different directions. The urge to move here and there never sitting still, is merely a physical reflection of the mind's inability to focus and remain calm in one place. People travel all over the world for happiness. Or, there are those who cannot stay in one job for very long, they need a change, excitement, variety, and are soon bored with their current environment. Many people are simply unable to sit still. Meditation enhances our ability to sit still in one position for an extended period of time. When the mind is tranquil, then so is the body.

Meditation develops our ability to remain tranquil and peaceful, to direct our every movement for a useful purpose. Rather than looking everywhere for satisfaction and finding nowhere, we are able to progress in any direction we choose with concentration and energy gained from this center.

Anahata Chakra

The fourth chakra is the *Anahata* chakra. *Anahata* means without being struck. It is the Heart Center; it is also the air center, since the element air is predominant in this chakra. It is the emotional center, where our feelings, our loves and hates, likes and dislikes as pairs of opposites arise.

This chakra is located in the spinal region at the middle of the chest in our subtle body. It contains the vital energy. Air is the vital life energy. Air is the symbol of stillness. Through breath control and self-control, yogis (meditators) regulate their life energy and are able to tread the path of inner peace. Heart remains the place of the main life force, which regulates the breath.

Through breath control, one gets mental and physical strength. The Heart Center circulates breath and is used continuously. Even when the body is resting, the heart center preserves life through the circulation of life energy.

The heart center controls our emotions. Our emotions can be the gauge of our maturity. Some people do not seem to mature with their ages. These people and all would benefit from meditation. The heart should be a place of love, instead of becoming a place of anger, ego, and pride.

By developing this center through meditation, we can energize this center—firstly by achieving needed the balance to deal with ups and downs of life, and secondly by channeling our emotions into a constructive course. Self-love, will be replaced with love for others, and release ourselves from self-made prison of our emotions. We will then be free without fear and restraint. Such a state can be achieved through meditation, relaxation, and self-inquiry. Some yoga practitioners emphasizing on the chakra meditation spend longer time meditating at the Heart Center.

The presiding deity of the heart center is Lord Vishnu, the maintainer and the sustainer of creation. It is a twelve-petal lotus. The subtle sound produced here is *yam*. Many believe that the presence of God is manifested more here than anywhere else in the body. One who meditates gain love and devotion to God.

Anahata chakra located at the middle of the seven chakras is also called the center of transformation. From here the mind can go down to the lower three centers, or travel upward to the upper three centers. The path of spirituality requires the transformation of passion to compassion and emotion to devotion. Sometimes people are transformed temporarily, but are pulled back by temptation and passion. But through regular practice of meditation and breath control, this transformation can become permanent.

Sense organs controlled by the heart center are skin (organ of touch) and hands (organ of work). The functions of the two sense organs improve and control develops.

Visuddha Chakra

The fifth chakra is known as *Visuddha,* located in the spine near the throat region. It is the center of religious and intellectual activities. Also through this center, people acquire love towards the creator (God). Most people use their skill and talent to achieve goals of their lives. Based on the tenets of a religion of choice, love towards God is developed at the *Visuddha* chakra. Over a period of time, the followers of a particular religion may become intolerant of other religions. This is perhaps natural and requires understanding among groups and faiths. Without love there can be no religion. All religions can be thought of as the petals of the same flower and one religion compliments another. Such an understanding is necessary and of primary importance for peace and harmony among nations.

Visuddha is a sixteen-petal lotus. Presiding deity is Lord Shiva. The seed syllable, which a meditator listen to is *sham* at this chakra.

Ajna Chakra

The sixth subtle energy center is known as the *Ajna* chakra, also known as the soul center. The center is located between the eyebrows, and five to seven cm inside the brain. This chakra is also known as the third eye. Concentration on here develops the self-control and the bad tendencies of the senses are defeated. *Ajna* chakra is a two-petal lotus; the presiding deity is the individual soul. The syllables produced at this center are *ham* and *ksham*.

Sahasrara Chakra

The seventh is the *Sahasrara* chakra situated at the top of the head in the fontanel, corresponding to the soft place at the scalp or a hole in the skull when one is newborn. The hole closes around three to four months of age leaving the fontanel associated with a hole in adults. The presiding deity at this chakra is the Supreme Self and the seed syllable *Om*, corresponding to a thousand petal lotus. Om sound is the combination of all sounds. The benefits of concentration are the attainment of more wisdom and realization of the Self.

Why Most People Ignore Meditation

Meditation is important and beneficial, one would think that everyone would jump into it, but we do not see that. It is the opposite that we see: there is hardly any interest in most people, let alone the younger people, who would get the most benefit out of meditation.

There are two groups of reasons:

1. **The forces of opposition in our minds;**
2. **We are not used to meditation from the beginning, that is, early years of our lives.**

The first group of reasons is elaborated allegorically in Bhagabad Gita, Chapter 1. Basically, there are forces of opposition in our minds. These forces prevent us from meditating. I will try to elaborate on the first group of reasons. The second group of reasons have been mentioned in another article—**Meditation for More Success and Happiness**. I refer the reader to that article.

The message in Gita is timeless and universal. The timeless message in Chapter 1 of Gita does not only refer to one historical battle, but also to the cosmic conflict between good and evil that goes on inside everyone. Sage Vyasa, the author of Gita was the Master in allegorical description. No words can adequately describe his capabilities.

Paramahamsa Yogananda in his Gita interpretations had shown that Chapter 1 of Gita is an allegory as was intended by sage Vyasa. He introduces allegorically the basic principles of the science of yoga and describes the initial spiritual struggle of a yogi.

In verse 1 of Chapter 1, the blind king Dhritarashtra is asking impartial Sanjaya: "on the holy plain of Kurukshetra, where my offspring (the Kurus) and the sons of Pandu (the Pandavas) had gathered together, eager for a battle, what did they do?"

Sage Vyasa uses past tense in asking Sanjaya to describe the battle. It is a clear indication that Gita is referring only incidentally to a historical battle in Kurukshetra. Primarily, Vyasa is describing a universal battle—the one that rages daily in man's life.

All characters involved in the battle have allegorical meanings. Dhritarashtra represents the blind mind; his sons Kurus represent the wicked mental and sense inclinations. Pandu represents the intellect, positive aspect of the mind. His sons, the Pandavas, represent the pure discriminative tendencies. The earnest question of the king Dhritarashtra is metaphorically the question every spiritual aspirant should ask as he reviews daily his own righteous battle from which he seeks the victory of Self-realization.

Everyday battle involves:
- **Self-control versus sense indulgence;**
- **Discriminative intelligence versus mental sense inclinations;**
- **Spiritual resolve in meditation versus mental resistance and physical restlessness; and**
- **Soul-consciousness versus ignorance, and attraction to the lower ego nature.**

Against the above daily hindrances, a strong determination is required for meditation.

The second verse refers to the strong material desire (king Duryodhana) that will bring in man's sense habit tendencies (instructor Drona) and impressions created by past thoughts and actions.

The third verse refers to the material desire and past habits encountering discriminative faculties (son of Drupada) ready to counteract (fight).

Verses 4, 5, and 6 describe the metaphysical soldiers of the soul that are aroused by meditation in preparation for the inner spiritual battle against those of the innate sense-habits of body identification of verses 7 and 8. The metaphysical soldiers of the soul are: devotion, samadhi, dispassion, mental resistance, spiritual memory, discriminative intelligence, internalization, right posture, and power of mental adherence, life force control, celibacy, Self-mastery, and the awakened spinal centers. The soldiers of the soul are to fight the sense habits represented by habit (samskaras), ego, attachment, individual delusion, latent desire, repulsion, karma, and body attachment.

Verses 9 and 10 refer to other diverse warriors and sense lures, those are abiding in the body to fight against the good. These are lust (kama), anger, greed, delusion, pride, and envy. The forces of desires and sense temptations are practically unlimited in number, but the combined strength may be inadequate because they all relate to the body identified state, whereas the soul forces, though limited in number, consist of the fundamental principles of the unchanging truth mentioned in the above paragraph.

In verse 11, king Duryodhana representing the material desire instructs the rest of the Kuru army (representing the mental and sense inclinations) to protect Bhishma, representing the ego, the consciousness of identifying with the body. If ego consciousness is defeated by army of meditation (discriminative forces of Pandava), the soul would get its perfect state and defeat the army of material desires.

In verse 12, ego consciousness (Bhishma) "blew his conch shell" of restless breath causing body identification and disrupting stillness of the meditative forces.

Verses 13-18 describe the psychological battle common in meditation through the vibratory sounds emanating from the sense tendencies on one side and the discriminative tendencies on the other side. In this battle, the physical and astral vibratory sound of the senses draws the consciousness towards the body. Opposite to that are the vibrations of the astral music, emitted by the inner discriminative powers and the vital activities of the spinal centers. This astral music draws the consciousness towards the soul and the spirit.

Most new meditators are unaware of the bodily and the discriminative astral vibrations. It is aim of this article to draw their attention to these important sound vibrations in the body, and ultimately listen to the Om sound current from the seventh chakra, *Sahasrara*.

Verse 19 is opposite to verse 12. The vibratory sounds emanating from the astral centers as heard during meditation discourages the body-bound mental and material desires and sense inclinations. The undisciplined mental tendencies automatically subside when a determined effort is made to practice meditation.

In verses 20-23, as the sounds from the astral centers discourages the body-bound mental tendencies; the devotee (the aspirant) hoists his flag of self-control (monkey emblem). It signifies man's control over restlessness. He lifts his "bow of meditation" straightening the spine by holding by his neck straight, pulling his shoulders back and pushing his chest forward and drawing his abdomen in.

In the initial stage of meditation, the mind is invariably occupied with sense objects and sense consciousness, and restless thoughts. Many people cannot overcome this psychological struggle between the senses and the soul forces of calmness and intuition.

Great determination of will is required to win the first inner psychological battle to keep the concentration steady and internalized. The devotee can get help if he recognizes the intimate interrelationship of the following four factors:

- Mind,
- Breath,
- Vital essence, and
- Bodily life energy

The devotee must calm the mind by right techniques of concentration, must keep the breath quiet by pranayama and proper breathing exercises, must preserve the vital essence by self-control and by seeking company of good people, and must free the body from restlessness and aimless motions by conscious control of the life force, and by keeping the body in good health.

Verses 24-25

When the good and evil in the spiritual aspirant are poised to fight during meditation, each side facing fierce struggle for victory, the uncertain devotee begins to rationalize what such a battle really means. The charioteer soul (one with the Spirit) places him face-to-face with the enemies he must destroy.

Verse 26

The enthusiastic spiritual beginner does not realize the power of resistance possessed by bad habits. Nor do the bad habits notice, at first, the silent invasion by good habits. It is only when the devotee gets serious and makes repeated struggles to establish the generals of good habits in the kingdom of consciousness that the generals of bad habits become alarmed and make furious attempts to oust the "intruders".

Verses 27-30

When the devotee has made some initial advances in his attempts with meditation, he is happy and satisfied. With further progress he finds that the sense desires are diehard inmates of his life. He begins to wonder, even in the midst of divine realization, if he has made the correct decision to forsake material joys for the sake of gaining spiritual happiness. He tries to split his allegiance—giving attention to the body and its sense enjoyments and part to the soul qualities. The result of these half measures is that the devotee's will power becomes less powerful. The taste of material habits dries up the taste of the subtle spiritual perceptions.

Verse 31

The devotee shows negative renunciation. He does not want to win over his bad traits and qualities. If he has to win over negative qualities, then he does not want his pleasures from his senses and sense inclinations. This is negative renunciation, equivalent to a child saying to his parents, "If I have to eat my carrots before I eat my ice cream, then I don't want my ice cream either!" The wise cosmic law is passively unmoved by the "heroic" display of negative renunciation.

In the mental uncertainty faced by a devotee after making initial spiritual progress, the devotee makes decision. He does not see any use in destroying all the sense comforts. He does not crave an empty mental victory leading to cosmic consciousness. He does not want sense happiness either.

Whenever the mind feels longing for the forsaken sense-pleasures, the devotee should instantly picture himself ending his pleasure-loving body—its eventual entry into the earth or the crematory flames.

Verses 32-34

The devotee bound by the habit of sensory experience clings subconsciously to the notion that the divine attainment enjoying the Kingdom of Heaven by the senses. In the light of his spiritual progress when he discovers that the soul forces are ready to destroy the material desires, his sensory conditioned logic begins to mislead him. He reasons that if he annihilates the ego consciousness and all gross sensory pleasures, desires, habits, in order to gain spiritual dominion over the bodily empire, the victory would be meaningless without the channels of sensory enjoyment.

Verses 35-39

The devotee argues that sense inclinations and bad habits should be kept even though they may destroy devotee's spiritual aspirations and progresses. **It is hard to give up sense pleasures of the present for unknown happiness that may come in the future with the regular practice of meditation. This is the reason people would rather**

live a life they are used to rather than learn the techniques of meditation and do regular practice and derive many benefits.

Devotee argues that destroying these sense habits would leave the life of devotee empty and be a sinful act. It is not the destruction of the actual senses, but to slay their bad habits. "When all sensory attachments—unwholesome lures of physical beauty, love of flattery and of words of temptation, bondage of greed, attraction of sex—are dislodged from matrices of the senses, it is then that the senses relinquish their material prejudices, inclinations, instincts, and obsessions; they become ready to be attached only to divine bliss."

The devotee also argues that sense habits are also the offspring of the mind. How could one benefit by destroying the senses, through which mind expresses itself. The devotee who suddenly becomes identified with the enemy (bad habits and moods) will find himself sympathizing with and justifying unwholesome actions.

Continue 38 and 39

The devotee argues that the pleasure-giving senses and the wisdom-bringing discrimination belong to the same family—they are the members of the devotee's consciousness. It is not reasonable to destroy the family clan of sense inclinations and the other set of discriminating inclinations should be allowed to live on.

The devotee believes that the sense-indulging habits could stay side-by-side with good habits. But it is impossible to have harmony and peace as long as contradictory forces work in one's life. The good habits and the bad habits, though they are the offspring of the same consciousness, manifest different results. **Those who equally enjoy sensory indulgence and meditational pleasures will not get anywhere for a long time.**

Verses 40-41

The meditating devotee advancing to a state of achievements towards his battle for Self-realization feels that all inclinations of the inner and outer members of the "family" of consciousness will be annihilated; and that without these inclinations with their desires for inner and outer objects, the specific functions of the senses, mind, vital forces, and intelligence will be lost.

The family refers to the inner and outer forces of cognition and expression through which the ego (or the soul in the enlightened man) is provided with a means of experiencing and interacting with the environment. The members of the family consist of the following:

- Five external senses giving powers of sight, hearing, smelling, tasting, and touching.
- Five organs of actions: power of speech, activities by hands and feet, reproduction, and elimination.
- Five vital live forces: metabolizing, circulatory, assimilating, eliminating, and crystallizing.
- Mind and intelligence.

The actions and interactions of these 17 inner and outer forces of perception, and their ego-guided or soul-governed reactions to the objects of perception, arouse in the devotee accordingly either good or evil inclinations.

The devotee's concern of losing the psychological members of his family is an expression of his apprehension about the new state of consciousness he is moving toward through practicing meditation. Contrary to his apprehension of losing the members of his family, in meditation (conscious contact of God) the inner and outer members of consciousness, though suspended, do not lose their individual powers or become distorted, instead, they are doubly recharged in perceptive power from the cosmic forces. The senses become rejuvenated and develop more subtle powers in expressing their individual characteristics.

Verses 42-43

Battle to destroy the senses: To withdraw in meditation the wisdom and life force that enlivens the senses.

The devotee continues to add new arguments to his same trend of rationalization. As he tries to make up his mind to engage in a battle to withdraw in meditation his life forces that enliven the senses, he now expresses his apprehension that his discriminative faculties may suffer disintegration owing to their lack of interaction with the senses. If the wisdom faculties are not utilized in the normal enjoyment of the senses, but are made to reside in the inner sanctum of the soul, will not the wisdom faculties along with the sense faculties be thrown into loneliness and meaningfulness?

The truth of the matter is quite the contrary. The negative feminine sense pleasures (the feeling or experiences of the senses) are guided by the positive masculine sense capabilities. If the masculine sense faculties—desire, material achievement, creative ability, initiative for material enjoyment—are destroyed in their battle with the discriminative faculties, then the feminine or "feeling" sense faculties—material pleasure, attachment, delusion, sense slavery—lose their "caste" consciousness of materiality and submit to the inner tendencies of the discriminative faculties. That is when the springs of the sense activities, sense desires, are destroyed; the feminine sense perceptions lose their material edge and guiding spirit, owing to the powerful influence of the discriminative tendencies. The whole clan of sense faculties thereby becomes not extinguished, but enlightened, by this domination of the wisdom faculties.

The ancestors of the family of human consciousness are the soul and its faculties of inner-seeing ego, and intuition. These ancestors are degraded into ordinary human sense consciousness unless they receive from the wisdom faculties a flow of inspiration and inwardly turned life force (water) and regular offerings of vital spiritual enthusiasm (rice balls). When the vitality of concentration and wisdom is developed, it inspires the soul and the intuitional powers; the inspired soul in turn reinforces the wisdom and intuition with all-seeing powers.

The advancing yogi, firm in meditative and self-control performs the true ancestral ceremony. He astrally (being the astral body) disconnects the life force from the sensory nerves. The yogi, firm in meditative and self-control; the life force begins to flow inward and, becoming focused at the point between the eyebrows, forms into an opalescent light. The inward astral flow and the inner light are the oblations of human wisdom to its ancestors of soul, divine ego, and intuition. Human wisdom must offer these vitalities to the soul faculties. Without the oblations of the inwardly flowing life force and spiritual perceptions, and the light of the spiritual eye, the soul faculties remain dormant, degradingly undeveloped.

Instead of being doubtful or despondent, the seeker of God should be glad to consign all sense pleasures to limbo in exchange for the lavish treasures of the soul.

Verses 44-46

The beginner yogi, forced to be quiet in meditation, often wonders if he is foolish enough to relinquish the tangible pleasures of the senses for a possible glimpse of the presently intangible pleasures of the Spirit. He feels disinclined to arm himself with austere laws of self-control. He thinks that his life will be sunk in constant misery by the destruction of the God-given sense pleasures, so easily available right now. He feels, it would be better for him to meet disillusionment and death from the senses rather than to be involved in a devastating battle between the discriminating forces and the sense inclinations.

In this state of mind the devotee is dissatisfied both because of his lack of spiritual progress and because of his long separation from his accustomed sense habits. At such time of his advancement in the spiritual path, he may childishly overreact by rebelling against all modes of self-control. The devotee should relax and not be too strict in disciplining the unruly child--his unconvinced mind. This state is finally overcome by partial renunciation and by reasonable effort in meditation, enjoying moderately wholesome sense pleasures.

The devotee should always keep in mind that the surrendering to the demands of the senses does not satisfy them, but rather creates insatiable desires for further sense experiences. Soul pleasures, though hard to attain, when once gained is never diminished; it knows no satiety; and yields ever new joys.

Most worldly people travel through life unarmed by any weapon of self-control and can meet disillusionment and death from the senses. The self-discipline demands not only of forsaking the indulgence of wrong pleasures, but also, the destruction of the thoughts of indulgence by the sense-sympathetic mind. He should think of the habitual desires as enemies in disguise. They promised him happiness, yet planned to give him only worries, insatiable longings, broken hopes, disillusionment and death. Although it is hard in the beginning to give up the kinds of material pleasures that obstruct the expression of the soul, renouncing such evil is his only hope of gaining lasting spiritual blessedness.

Verse 47

When the devotee does not have a sufficient spiritual power to quiet his doubts, he feels himself to be a weakling and unfit for the psychological inner battle. Full of grief and casting away his divine weapons of bow of meditation and the arrows of inner powers, he indifferently settles down on the chariot of intuitive perception. The chariot represents the vehicle in which the devotee's discriminative forces engage in psychological and metaphysical battle with the senses.

If the devotee does not progress, it is because he discards his weapons of self-control; a discouraged devotee often gives up all self-discipline when he does not attain spectacular progress in the spiritual path. The devotee should practice meditation regularly, and show discrimination against the lures by the senses.

The first chapter of Gita refers to the sorrows involved in the devotee's initial effort to attain yogic union with God.

Meditation for Success
and Happiness

Salutation to my spiritual master!

It is the Master who speaks through the disciples.

I am not a master or a guru. I am just an humble student on meditation. I found it very helpful, and would like to pass along some knowledge or experiences. Hence this talk I am giving you today.

Ask anyone who meditates regularly or even occasionally, "Is meditation beneficial? Do you find it useful?" I am sure; you will hear an affirmative answer that meditation is beneficial for our living.

Lord Krishna mentions about meditation in many verses of Gita, and, in particular, in Chapter 6 He elaborates meditation practices. It is a technique for improving ourselves spiritually to understand our true Self: free, immortal, spiritual being. But on the way there are many benefits for worldly living.

Many people might say, "I have many problems at hand. Or, I am very busy. I have no time to meditate." If the person would have meditated, he might not have such a response. However, the truth is that even though our ultimate purpose is to find our way back to God, but we also have a task to perform in this world.

How best can you do your job in this world? That is the question I would like to explore through discussion of the benefits of meditation, particularly, with respect to success and happiness.

In this world and in the society, God has placed each of us in particular places and in particular circumstances. We according to our own karma, evolution, education, talents and abilities, earn our living. Can everyone become millionaire or multi-millionaire? It may or may not be possible. But can everyone improve their lot under whatever conditions they are in and become more successful and happier? The answer is firmly "Yes". If you simply meditate regularly, you can achieve this modest goal. It is that simple.

Babaji (dearly father) Nagaraj, the great, immortal (literally), eternally youth, Himalayan yoga Master advised one of his direct disciples of the 20th century, **"I want you to grow up as an integrated, calm, steady, stable individual. Give yourself to the inner man; then you can meet the challenge of any man, anywhere, and everywhere."** Very valuable advice, please keep this in mind.

This advice is applicable to everyone. We have to give ourselves to the inner man – this means we have to go deep inside ourselves and meditate. If we do that regularly, then we can meet the challenge of any man, anywhere, and everywhere. This is the secret: control your mind. Mind is said to be a terrible master, but a very good servant. Meditation unlocks all potential power in an individual. You do not know your power until you regularly meditate.

It is easy to meditate: simply sit down quietly and follow a technique for achieving concentrations. But why don't people in general meditate? The majority of us do not show any enthusiasm in learning and practicing meditations. There are two kinds of reasons of for doing so.

The first group of reasons is elaborated allegorically in Gita, Chapter 1. Basically, there are forces of opposition in our minds. These forces prevent us from meditating or taking the right endeavors for our wellbeing. The first group of reasons has been discussed in another article—Meditation-Why Most People Ignore Meditation?

The second group of reasons arises from the fact that we are not used to meditation in the form of a habit from the childhood. Anything we are not used to from our childhood is kind of foreign to us. Unless we are forced to learn something as we do in schools and colleges, we do not usually learn it.

Those of us, who are serious about meditation, happened to come to know it almost by chance. We are ever so grateful for that. People in general are more of devotees than they are of yogis. That is of course the Bhakti Yoga, the path of devotion, very much elaborated in Gita, Chapter 12, in particular. But also, the path of meditation has been also elaborated equally well if not more in Gita. Whole Chapter 6 in Gita is about meditation. There are numerous mentions about meditation in almost all chapters of Gita. Then why do we go more towards path of devotion than towards the path of meditation?

From the very childhood, we go to temple with elders, bow down to God and deities, perform worshipping ceremonies (pujas), and participate in various programs: religious and cultural, listen to devotional music, and take *prasadam* (sanctified food offered to the Lord). These are all rituals of the Bhakti Yoga or the path of devotion. Thus the path of devotion gets into our habits. This gets ingrained in our thoughts and activities. On the other hand, there are practically no programs or rituals that teach us to meditate from the beginning of our childhood. This is the point we have to pay attention to.

I think it is fair to say that if we were exposed to meditation from our childhood, we would meditate more than we do now as a group. There have to have programs in which children can get exposed to meditation. Can we think of introducing a meditation program to our youths? I am sure that our youths would be very much thankful to us for that in the future when the youths realize the benefits of the early start of meditation. This is the age you can mold them into anything, particularly, if it is that good like meditation. This is a big opportunity. The benefit of meditation will self-perpetuate the program.

This is a very competitive world. Our youths need an extra tool. Meditation will be an extra tool for them. Meditation along with devotion will put you in the right course of your life.

In childhood and youth years, you are a celibate. You have not entered into the life of a householder. You are an idealist, optimist; you do not know the complexities of the world. Thus, a youth should be able to learn meditation easily and get all the benefits from meditation; in particular, if there are programs, where they are exposed to in their childhood years.

How do you become more successful?

Now let us see how meditation can help us to become more successful and happier?

Let us consider the following:

#1 The success in life does not altogether depend on ability and training; it also depends on our determination to grasp opportunities that are presented to us. Opportunities in life come by creation, not by chance. We ourselves either now or in the past (past lives) have created all opportunities that arise in our path. Since we created them, use them to the best advantage.

We demonstrate success or failure according to our habitual trend of thought. If our mind is ordinarily in the negative state, an occasional positive thought is not sufficient. If we think rightly, we will find our goal even though we seem to be enveloped in darkness.

Let us not mentally review our problems constantly. At times, take rest. Use this rest period to go deep within the calm region of our inner

Self. Attuned with the soul, we will be able to think correctly regarding everything we do.

Several qualities of success: positive thoughts, dynamic will, self-analysis, and self-control. In addition to these, there is another most important attribute to success: It is the Divine Will. Attunement with the Divine Will is the most important factor in attracting success. It is the power that moves the cosmos and everything in it.

Through meditation techniques, one can be in harmony of the Divine Will.

The power of divine attunement can be achieved by practice of meditation and concentration efforts.

#2 Just as all power lies in His will, so all spiritual and material gifts flow from His boundless abundance. In order to receive His gifts, we must eradicate from our mind all thoughts of limitations and poverty.

The confidence and consciousness of abundance are attained through meditation. Since God is the source of all mental power, peace, and prosperity, first contact God. Thus we may harness our will and activity to achieve the highest goals

By the power of concentration and meditation, we can direct the inexhaustible power of our minds to accomplish what we desire and to guard every door against failure.

#3 Keep your mind centered on the thought of God – source of all power and all accomplishment. The ability to center the mind in thoughts of God is achieved through the practices of meditation.

Mind is the creator of everything. We should therefore guide it to create only the good. If we cling to certain thoughts with dynamic will power, it finally assumes a tangible outward form. When we are able to employ our will for constructive purposes, we become the controllers of our destiny.

Along with the positive thinking we should use our will power, and continuous activity to be successful. Will power is the spring of all actions. Conscious or dynamic will power is the one needed for getting a job done one thing at a time.

We should always be sure within the calm region of our inner Self, that what we want is right for us to have, and in accord with God's purposes.

#4 Mental habits are shaped by meditation. Success is hastened or delayed by one's habits. Mental habits control our lives. Habits of thoughts are mental magnets that draw to us certain things, people, and conditions. Good habits of thoughts enable us to attract benefits and opportunities. Bad habits of thoughts attract us to unfavorable environments.

Take initiative for doing something. Initiative is a creative faculty within a person, a spark of the Infinite Creator and a great inventive power of the Spirit. It may give you the power to create something no one has ever created.

Happiness

Happiness depends to some extent on the external conditions, but mainly upon mental attitudes. In order to be happy one should have good health, a well-balanced mind, a prosperous life, the right work, a thankful heart, and above all wisdom or knowledge of God.

If you possess happiness, you possess everything: to be happy is to be in tune with God. That power to be happy comes through meditation.

If you possess health and wealth, but have trouble with others, including you, yours is not a successful life. Existence becomes futile if you cannot find happiness. Success therefore should be measured by the yardstick of happiness, by our ability to remain in harmony with the cosmic laws.

God does not reward or punish anyone. He has given us the power to reward or punish us by the use or misuse of our own reason and will power. We should strengthen our minds and refuse to carry the burden of mental and moral weaknesses acquired in the past years, burn them in the fires of our present divine resolutions and right activities.

All people cannot play the same role. Someone's work may be very humble and modest. He has to keep in mind that he is just fulfilling the duty given by the Lord. God needs him in that particular place. So long as he works to please God, all cosmic forces will harmoniously assist him. When you convince God that you want Him above all else, you will be tuned to His will.

Let us all resolve to put our little efforts to meditation, be more successful and be happier.

Teachings of Bhagavad Gita in Day to Day Life

Who are we?

We are all parts of the Divine. Our life-sparks – our souls – come from God. We are living in God now and we always live in God. We are spiritual beings. We have the Divine heritage. Upon taking birth we come in contact with what is called material contamination. Under the influence of God's energy of Maya, we forget, ignore, or disregard our Divine roots. Thus, we start our lives in this physical world.

Because of our Divine heritage, we have the inherent tendency to show our unhappiness with material things and look for spiritual happiness. This is the Divine play. We must become perfect. God has provided us our body temples and all the necessary items to go back to Godhead. This is the aim of our lives behind whatever we do for living in this physical world. God has given us also our free will. We must use our free will to lead a wholesome life and move closer and closer to Godliness. Even if we do not willingly make efforts in this incarnation, we are destined to make efforts eventually. We all will be liberated from the flawed perceptions of the material world and come to the understanding of the Omnipresence God—this is the Divine play.

Our real nature is *Sat-Chit-Ananda* – Existence, Consciousness, and Bliss. That is what God is. We have come from God, and our ultimate destiny is to return to Him. At the soul level, we are all the same despite our apparent differences.

Why do we need Gita?

Gita is the summation of all our scriptures: *Vedas*, *Upanishads*, and all the major systems of Hindu philosophy. It is said that the entire knowledge of the Cosmos is parked into the Gita.

Gita is our link of the present with the past and the future. People throughout the ages received inspiration from Gita and understood Gita in their own personal ways. Many have written interpretations of Gita. This has been continuing in the past, present, and will continue in the future.

The teachings of Gita start from the battlefield. One can take the battle literally to have taken place between the good and the bad. One can take the battle figuratively between the good and the bad tendencies inside us. Whatever the battle we must fight, we will have the determination not to succumb to the evil forces. This fundamental teaching of Gita will help tremendously in our lives.

Life is a continuous battle from the moment of conception to old age and death. The first contest of the soul in each incarnation is with other souls seeking rebirth. Human life is thus rare indeed. It is a great opportunity for us to move further ahead.

After each struggle, we have to move forward learning new things for betterment of our souls reclaiming inch by inch the territories of the soul occupied by ignorance.

Gita tells us that we must work. In fact, no one can sit idle. Everything in the universe from minutest nuclear particles to the entire universe is in motion. Gita tells us that we have to do our duty steadfastly without aspiring to the fruits of our actions. Do not act for selfish reasons. Do not get attached to inaction. Dedicate your action to the Lord. If we can do that we do not create *karma* and move towards liberation. This is how karma becomes *karma yoga*. Attachments disturb peace, leads to bondage, and create *karma* for the next incarnation.

Gita tells us we are immortal souls, nothing can kill us. This assurance gives us the peace of mind if we can understand and assimilate the teachings in us. Lord tells not to grieve for the dead. Birth and death are continuous cycles until we are fully awakened to God.

In Gita Lord Krishna declares He is the Supreme God. If we do worship other form of gods and goddesses, the worship reaches the Supreme God.

Gita tells us how to live properly for spiritual advancement and how to die keeping concentration between the eyebrows and thinking of the Divine.

Gita tells us to practice detachments. In spite of all the attachments we have, each one of us on our own – we are always in the infinite. No one else can think our thoughts, dream our noble dreams. Our guru can give us a seed *mantra* or a technique to practice Mantra repetition. We have to try hard and become realized on our own efforts and initiative.

Desire and anger in us cause damage to our inner peace.

What is the best form of happiness? Supreme peace comes to a yogi, whose mind is quiet and peaceful, whose passion is quieted, and who is free from sin and has become *Brahman* (meaning the Absolute in Sanskrit).

This brings us to controlling of the mind and techniques of meditation. One whole Chapter 6 deals with meditation. There are numerous mentions of meditation or yoga in the Gita. Lord Krishna tells Arjuna a Yogi is greater than an ascetic, better than a man of wisdom, superior to those who are devoted to the path of action.

Verse 13 in Chapter 6 has been misinterpreted by many commentators of Gita. Paramahamsa Yogananda has pointed this out in his Gita interpretations.

Translation of the verse is as follows: One should hold one's body, neck head in a straight line, and focus his gaze at the origin of the nose without looking around and keeping the mind undistracted.

Nasikagram in the verse 6.13 means start of the nose and not tip of the nose. One has to concentrate at the location of the start of the nose not at the tip of nose. There are no techniques for meditation that instruct one to stare at the tip of the nose. This becomes clear from the verse 8:12, which clearly says to concentrate between the eyebrows. The translation is as follows: Having restrained all the senses, drawing the mind into the heart, and keeping the *Pranas* (concentration) centered at the space between the eyebrows, steady in the practice of Yogic concentration.

Gita verses 29-30 of Chapter 4 and verses 27-28 of Chapter 5 refers to the techniques of Kriya Yoga meditation, which is a form of Raja Yoga. It is very popular and effective meditation technique. The techniques of meditation are said to be the direct route to approaching Godliness. Babaji (also known as *Kriya Babaji*) initiated Lahiri Mahasaya to Kriya Yoga in 1861. Please refer to my article on Babaji Nagaraj. In the same lineage, the present (2017) Kriya Master is *Paramahamsa Prajnanananda*.

Everyone should do meditation as emphasized in Gita. In particular, the younger generation should learn the techniques (not necessarily, Kriya yoga) from qualified teachers and practice diligently. It is a lifelong technique to practice. There are always ladders to climb with many benefits. Meditation removes boredom and loneliness. The practice of meditation should accompany some physical exercises.

We learn from Gita (chapter 14 and other chapters) that people, food, action, and giving are all of three types: *sattva*, *rajas* and *tamas*. We have to choose the *sattvic* way of life. *Sattva* means purity, *rajas* means passion, and *tamas* means inertia. After becoming *sattvic*, we have to go above these three qualities.

Several Gita verses, 4.24, 15.14, and 9.27, are recited as a form of prayer to the Lord during meal times. The translation of these verses is as follows:

> 4.24. One sees *Brahman* (the Absolute) as the offering, *Brahman* as the clarified butter to be offered into the fire of *Brahman* by *Brahman* himself; he verily holds the perpetual vision of *Brahman* in action.
>
> 15.14. Having become the digestive fire, it is I who abide in all living beings, and having been united with Prana (outgoing breath) and Apana (incoming breath), it is I who digest four kinds of food.
>
> 9.27. Whatever you do, whatever you eat, whatever you offer or give away, whatever austerities you perform, do that O son of Kunti, as an offering to Me

The task of getting liberation is not easy. It requires efforts of many life times. Spiritual path is said by the wise to be razor thin. There are many pitfalls on the way. However, if one falls from the spiritual path, that is not the end. Lord promises that the person falling from the spiritual path starts again from the position where he deviated from in the past.

Our eternal home is the subtle or the astral world. We spend a very small fraction of our time in the physical world. During the period we are here, we have to strive to be Self- and God realized. Until we are realized we have to try to act and behave like we are. This will enhance the process.

The whole of the Bhagavad-Gita is full of teachings suitable for day to day living. The above is a small attempt to enumerate or point out a few of them. Let us start following some teachings from Gita in our lives.

Advice to Teenagers and Younger Generation

Chapter 16, verses 1-3 mention of many qualities the younger generation should pursue. Some of these are fearlessness, purity of the mind, steadfastness, control of the senses, sacrifice, study of the scriptures, straightforwardness, etc. Teenagers must learn to channel well their mental and physical energies. They should guard against the wastage of inner strength in mere sense pleasures.

Divine Mother

Trying to Understand the Divine Mother

I bow down to Mother Durga, remover of all troubles and worries.

Let us try to understand Mother Durga, and the Divine Mother. How is the Divine Mother manifested in the world?

Mother Durga is an aspect (expression) of the Divine Mother — representing energy or shakti, the female creative force personified. Divine Mother is connected to the Infinite God, and Mother Durga is an expression of the Divine Mother, so, Mother Durga is also the Divine Mother.

Who is Divine Mother? We have to go little deeper to understand.

How do we know that the power of the Divine Mother is operative in our lives and everywhere else?

Let me start with the Absolute Reality of the universe—*Brahman*, the Source. The Absolute is without any qualities, and is inconceivable. *Brahman* is non-responsive, and completely and totally indifferent to the existence of the worlds, which originated from His being.

The moment we give *Brahman* an attribute (a quality); there is a response from the Absolute. The response comes because God (the Absolute with attributes) is existence, consciousness, bliss. Our consciousness dwells in the brain and the heart. God's consciousness dwells in the universe. Our consciousness is felt in the body; God's consciousness dwells in every unit-cell of space.

The earthly existence of our immortal Self in a physical body begins through the conception by our mothers. It is only natural that we long to have continuing care from our mothers, and plead and pray to God in the form of the Divine Mother for help and guidance. God responds and the grace of the Divine Mother is showered on us. God takes care of us all in the form of the Divine Mother. God has no gender. Whatever attribute we give to Him that is how our relationship with Him starts.

Saints have prayed to God to manifest as the Divine Mother or in the form of various deities. When an advanced devotee's devotion is strong enough to persuade God to materialize Himself in some specific aspect as imagined by the devotee, the form assumed by that deity remains in the ether as a permanent blueprint and personality. These deities subsequently can be invoked by any seeker in deep meditation.

Where there is love, compassion, and mercy whatever sources they come from, the direct presence of the Divine Mother can be felt. She is the nurturing influence we all need at every stage of our lives. *Paramahamsa Yogananda*, the great yogi and spiritual giant, lost his mother when he was 11 years old. He heard the Divine Mother consoling him, "It is I who have watched over you life after life in the tenderness of many mothers. See in My Gaze, the two black eyes, the lost beautiful eyes, you seek". Divine Mother takes care of all of us, in fact, all the creation.

God in action, God in love with His creation is the Divine Mother. God as redeemer of the humanity, maintainer and sustainer of all creatures and the liberator of the soul is the Divine Mother.

There was never a time, She did not exist. She is that aspect of the Divine which is immanent and accessible. In one description of the Mother, she has a necklace, on the necklace there are millions of beads. Each bead contains all the ages of the universes. Millions of times, the universe was created and dissolved, recreated and re-dissolved. Who is the Divine Mother? The Lady on whose person this necklace is.

We worship the Mother Durga, the female creative force personified in the form of an icon. A deeper meaning of the icon of Mother Durga is the following:

Mother Durga is depicted with 10 hands, representing 10 human senses: 5 sensory instruments (sight, hearing, smell, taste, and touch) and 5 instruments of actions (hands, feet, speech, organs of reproduction, and elimination). She is associated with Lord Shiva, the Infinite, and is shown destroying a demon that symbolizes Ignorance. She is surrounded by deities, her children: Saraswati (wisdom), Lakshmi (prosperity), Ganesh (success), and Kartik (power). The symbolism of the icon of Mother Durga means: **When senses are controlled and the demon of ignorance is conquered, and the person acquires desirable qualities and realizes the Cosmic Nature. This is exactly what one can achieve through meditation. So, the icon of Mother Durga can be considered to represent a visual expression of what meditation is.**

The martial form of Mother Durga—the Divine Mother—is inherited by each one of us. This quality maybe more pronounced in some than in others. So worshipping of the Divine Mother should bring in our intense desire to arise our fighting abilities. Every moment of our life is a struggle. We are battling both inside and outside forces. Some of the forces are evil and must be won over. We are immortal beings, and playing our parts with our body-mind constitutions. The essence of our existence is godly and immortal. To restore to our essence of beings, we must win over our negative mental tendencies and our egocentric inclinations. To go past our ordinary human endeavors, we must, however, try to understand the icon of the Divine Mother and bring in meditative qualities to control our senses and slay the demon of ignorance within us.

In India, the martial form of the Divine Mother—Mother Durga came to symbolize the country. The symbolism was strongly aided by the Bande Mataram (I worship the mother) song of Bankim Chandra. People's love and devotion poured out for mother India through the love of the Divine Mother. The feelings of people were expressed through the worshipping of the martial form of Mother Durga. Today's renewed pomp and grandeur in the observance of the Durga Puja festival in India and elsewhere surely indicate people's earnest prayer to the Divine Mother to come to the rescue of the humanity from evil forces. Surely, the Divine Mother is the mother of all, not of just India and Indian people, but in fact of the whole world and the cosmos.

It is the bound duty of all of us to propitiate the Divine Mother for she rules supreme over the health and wealth of the universe. That is why we worship the Divine Mother in the form of Mother Durga.

Prayer to the Divine Mother:
> tvameva maata cha pita tvameva tvameva bandhuschcha sakhaa tvameva
> tvameva vidya dravinam tvameva tvameva sarvam mama devadeva

Translation: You are my mother, father, friend, and beloved. You are my knowledge, you are my treasure, and you are everything I have.

Shiva the Lord

I would like to start with a quotation from the great Saivaite saint Yogaswmi, the Satguru of Subramuniyaswami of the Hawaii Hindu Monastery. "Know thy Self by thyself. Shiva is doing it all. All is Shiva. Be still."

Ordinarily when people say Yoga, they mean what is known as Hatha Yoga. It consists of physical exercises. Hatha Yoga is entirely different from Yoga, in the true sense of the word. The word Yoga means union with God. And, God is our higher self. So, Yoga leads to rediscovering of ourselves and, this means, Yoga leads to Self realization or God realization. This is the goal behind everything we do. Also, to emphasize is the fact that Yoga consists of some techniques of meditation. Therefore, Yoga is a scientific process for God realization. More mundane achievements on the way are calmness, better health, appreciation for living, and increasingly higher level of consciousness. Mere blind practices of the techniques will lead to wonderful results. However, not all teachings of Yoga are the same. Some are more powerful than others are.

Lord Shiva is the originator of Yoga and is the Lord of the Yogis. He is always shown in a meditative pose, known as the Shambhavi Mudra or open-eyed meditation. Many famous Yoga Masters are shown in this pose. They are Babaji, Lahiri Mahasaya, and Sri Yukteshwara. Shambhavi Mudra is an unfocused look into the infinity. A divine milky white light is observed during this meditation process. A student of Kriya Yoga routinely practices Shambhavi Mudra as a part of the Kriya mediation process.

Lord Shiva as Yogi very appropriately resides in the Himalayas, specifically at the Mount Kailash there. There is an inner meaning associated with Lord Shiva's leaving in the Himalayas. *Hima* means cold, and *Alaya* means the abode. When our mind is cool, not agitated, irritated or turbulent we reach the abode of Lord Shiva. Shiva is present in the internal Himalayas within all of us.

Now let us see where are the internal Himalayas? Lord Shiva (Supreme Self) is said to reside in the uppermost chakra – Sahasrara- at the fontanel near the pineal gland. This is the Center for Cosmic Consciousness. There are seven chakras located in our subtle bodies along the spinal pathway. Chakras are psycho-energy centers along the spine, very important to a student of Yoga. At the base of the spine is the Muladhar chakra. The second chackra from the base is Swadhisthana. Parvati, the consort of Shiva, resides at the second chackra. Muladhar chakra represents the primordial energy. This energy is also known as the Kundalini Shakti.

By various yogic processes it is possible to awaken the Kundalini energy. In particular, Kriya Yoga meditation is very effective in awakening the Kundalini energy gently. Kriya yoga is just another name of Raja Yoga.

Kundalini just awakened—difficult to control—is referred by the 18 Siddhas (accomplished persons) of South India as the Goddess Kali Devi. When Kundalini power can be controlled, it brings peace and beatitude or profound bliss. This has been referred to as Goddess Durga. When awakened Kundalini reaches the Sahasrara chakra, and *Nirvikalpa* samadhi, an un-fluctuating state of the highest level of consciousness, unfolds. Siddhas referred to this as the union of Shiva and Parvati Shakti. The seer, the process of seeing, and the object seen merge into one.

The Third Eye of Lord Shiva is prominent. I think there are many stories on Lord Shiva's third eye. Everyone has a third eye, also known as the Spiritual Eye or Spiritual Center. It is located in between the eyebrows little inside near the pituitary gland (Ajna chakra). It is the center of intuition (or the 6th sense). From this center, intuition or perfect knowledge comes from. The third eye is developed through development of univision by rigorous practices of meditation, in particular meditation at the Ajna Chakra between the eyebrows.

I will conclude this talk by giving a quotation in praise of meditation from Babaji, the original Master of Kriya Yoga meditation, and still living on the physical plane. This was originally addressed to V. T. Neelakantan before whom Babaji appeared, but applies to all of us. "I want you to grow up as an integrated, calm, steady, stable individual. Give yourself to the 'inner man', then, you can meet the challenge of any man, anywhere and everywhere. Don't go in to ruminate, but get in and dominate. Will you?"

Experiences with Baba Hariharananda

I received initiation into *Kriya* yoga and blessings from Baba *Paramahamsa Hariharananda* on February 13, 1999 at the *Kriya* Yoga Institute, Homestead, Florida. Swami *Vidyadhishanandaji* performed the initiation ceremony. This was the culmination of years of preparation on my part, and climbing of many spiritual ladders towards this attainment. Let me explain.

During my childhood and youth years in the present-day Bangladesh I was devotional. I visited along with my family many temples and holy men (sadhus). My family for a few generations has been the devotee of Baba *Lokenath Brahmachari* (1730-1890), a great yogi, who settled in the village of Baradi, not far from my birthplace (Araihazar). Baba Lokenath lived at Baradi for 26 years before his *mahasamadhi* (passing). At some stage of my youth years, I used to read daily verses from the Gita. After graduation from college, I came to the West for higher studies. Soon I became fully involved in life to be a materialist. At the time I was studying in the West in late sixties and early seventies, there were not many temples and opportunities like available today to get exposures to teachings of my religion, Hinduism.

When I settled down in the College Station (Texas) area, I came to know of *"Hinduism Today"*, a magazine published at the Hindu Monastery of Hawaii by *Satguru Sivaya Subramuniyaswami*. *Swamiji* as the founder of the monastery and through publication of this popular magazine contributed extensively to the Hindu renaissance movement. I happened to be subscribing this magazine for a long time now. The magazine has been extremely helpful for me in getting current information on organizations, temples, and events involving Hinduism or Hindu scriptures. In response to my letter to the monastery, I was very fortunate to receive a reply from *Satguru Sivaya Subramuniyaswami.*

A tragedy befell on us. Our twenty-year-old son, a Stanford student, passed away on May 7, 1996. It dawned on me that my life style had to change. One of our friends, a devotee of *Sai Baba,* advised us to visit *Sai Baba* in India. I made a pilgrimage along with my family to *Sathya Sai Baba* and had his holy *darshan* (seeing). I strongly believe that this visit helped me to make progresses in my spiritual journey.

I was already meditating following the basic techniques for some years, when I came to know about *Autobiography of a Yogi* by *Paramahamsa Yogananda* and his other books through advertisements in *Hinduism Today* by the Self Realization Fellowship (SRF), organization founded by Yoganandaji. I read the autobiography and later I bought the 2-volume set of *God Talks with Arjuna -The Bhagavad Gita* by *Yoganandaji.* I wrote a letter to

Daya Mata of the SRF. *Mataji* (dearly mother) was very kind to reply my letter, and offered me a very uplifting and valuable spiritual advice. A portion of this letter I am quoting below:

> Every stage of spiritual development is achieved by the grace of God, the blessings of the Guru, and the disciple's loyal practice of the Guru's teachings. Everything comes in time. But the goal is not to leave the body, but rather to live in tune with God and immersed in His love. Then He will add to the devotee whatever is for his highest good. Receive my divine love and prayer for your own spiritual progress. *Sri Daya Mata."*

Reading from *Yoganandaji,* I have been very fascinated and enchanted by Babaji, the *Kriya Mulaguru* (the Original Master), and all the *Kriya* yoga Masters. Over the years, I read two more books on *Babaji* published by *Babaji's Kriya Yoga Order of Acharyas,* Quebec, Canada. Also, I came to know of the Center for Spiritual Awareness (CSA), organization led by Mr. Roy Eugene Davis, a direct disciple of Yoganandaji. I contacted the CSA, purchased few books and a tape on the basic techniques of meditation. I found the books and publications of CSA very much enlightening on *Kriya* yoga and meditation in general, right living, and God concepts. I felt strongly that I should learn more about *Kriya* yoga. Later on, I received initiation from Mr. Davis during a ceremony at a Dallas hotel. I started receiving the *Truth Journal* magazine published by CSA. I believe this magazine and books I got from CSA have been very helpful for my spiritual progress.

I also came to know through *Hinduism Today* of an Indian saint living in Austria. He was Swami *Omkaranandaji*, a disciple of Swami *Shivananda* of Rishikesh, India. There was an article on *Swamiji* and his hermitages in Austria and Switzerland. I was very much attracted to Omkaranandaji and felt that it was the opportunity for me to receive *mantra diksha* (initiation). I traveled to Austria and Switzerland along with my wife and daughter. I received mantra initiation from Swami *Omkaranandaji*.

During the time I was practicing *Kriya* yoga meditation and *pranayama* (control breathing) as was taught by Mr. Roy Eugene Davis of the CSA, I came to know of Baba of the *Kriya* Yoga Institute at Homestead, Florida. Again it was through *Hinduism Today*. There appeared advertisements in several issues of the magazine with a picture of Baba *Hariharananda*. I thought this was a picture of a western Swami. The divine and loving appearance of Baba attracted me very much. Later on, there was an article by Baba also published in one issue of the magazine. In that article, Baba wrote about short breathing during *Kriya* meditation: short breaths were essential for achieving spiritual progress in meditation. Short breaths seemed mysterious and I wanted to learn the techniques.

I contacted the Kriya Yoga Institute by telephone and expressed interest in learning meditation and breathing techniques from Baba. I received contact information of a disciple of the *Kriya* Yoga Center at Dallas, Texas. I was strongly advised that if I wanted to learn *Kriya* yoga, I had to go and meet Baba soon. Baba was in his nineties and might not be physically present long.

I made a trip to the *Kriya* Yoga Institute on Friday, February 12, 1999. Swami *Vidyadhishanandaji* talked to me upon my arrival there and instructed me immediately to watch a video on *Kriya* yoga in the afternoon. I met Baba as he came out in the late afternoon from his room and was moving around in a wheel chair in the institute gardens. I bowed down to Baba and introduced myself. Then Baba also introduced himself. I told him that I knew him. He asked me how I came to I know him. I told him that I read about him.

In the evening I was allowed to participate in the daily evening meditation (even though I was not an initiate at that time) guided by *Vidyadhishanandaji*. I participated with enthusiasm, and also watched for the first time the meditation techniques that came down in succession from *Babaji* to Baba *Hariharananda* and to us.

I got accommodation at the guesthouse at 152nd Avenue at Homestead, Florida along with few others. The guesthouse was about six miles from the Institute.

The next morning (Saturday February 13, 1999) I received initiation into *Kriya* yoga from *Vidyadhishanandaji* following an elaborate ritual. There were six new initiates that morning. After the initiation, we came to Baba for blessings. He touched me and talked to me. He told me that his father's name was the same as mine. He asked me what part of West Bengal I was from. I told him that I was born in Bangladesh, and that my immediate family was living at the Ranaghat area in West Bengal. Baba knew Ranaghat well, and remembered his birthplace, which was not very far from Ranaghat area. I remember Baba was impressed with one of the new initiates who had a good physique and Christ like appearance. When his turn came to come near Baba, he (Baba) told him patting his shoulder that he was 1 in 500, 1 in 1000, or even 1 in 5,000. It was inspiring to see Baba praising someone.

In the afternoon, we learnt the techniques of *Kriya* yoga meditation from *Vidyadhishanandaji*. Following the technique session, we participated in the evening meditation session. On Sunday morning, I participated a meditation session guided by Baba. Sunday afternoon, we again went to Baba's room. This time, all those present in the Institute went to Baba for blessings. Baba was lying on the bed, and we one by one came near him and bowed down to his lotus feet. After I finished my bow, he pointed out the pictures on a nearby table. In particular, he mentioned about two pictures. One picture was that of Shri Bijoy Krishna Chattapadhyaya, the great householder renunciate, who influenced Baba's early life. The other picture was of Mira Bai., the sixteenth century consummate devotee of Lord Krishna.

In the evening there was another session on meditation, which I participated. I was not a strong person. Not having enough rest after arduous meditation sessions, my body reacted unfavorably to the new meditation techniques and for probably not doing them correctly. I was exhausted. Monday morning, I had to get up 4:00 AM to take a limousine to Miami airport to avail myself of an early morning flight to Houston and then to College Station.

Starting somewhat late in my life, I became a regular practitioner of *Kriya* yoga realizing that God has given me this opportunity, and I must do my best to excel in this meditation technique.

In early 2002, I was in a very difficult situation with a business party, my company was supposed to be merging with. It put me under considerable stress and strain. It continued for months of uncertainty with legal expenses. I always wondered during this difficult period, how come I have been thrust into this situation? The Prajnana Mission publication,

Sthita Prajna and a few publications from CSA, in particular, the *Truth Journal*, were helpful for me to provide some clues that comforted me. I learnt to start praying regularly. This I did not do regularly before. Every morning and evening during my prayer or recitation of few Sanskrit verses, I remember Baba along with other Masters who came to life.

I wrote a letter to Baba explaining my situation and requesting his blessings in that difficult time. I also wondered in that letter if I was trying to escape my problems requesting his blessings at that time. After some time, I received an email from Baba on September 12, 2002, about three months before Baba's *mahasamadhi* (passing).

The letter is as follows:

"My affectionate and divine Haripada Dhar,
      I am extremely happy to receive your letter.
      God is constantly with you in your whole body. You should search him with short breath and your fulfillment will be fulfilled. He is always within you and in everybody and everywhere.
      Search Him with short breath, and then you will get everything.
      My affection and blessings are always with you all.

                                             Humble,
                                             Hariharananda"

My personal situation gradually improved. By middle of 2003, the situation came under control, and I was calmed.

I am ever so grateful to the spiritual Masters, who came to my life through God's grace. Baba *Hariharananda* taught, *"Guru's glory is indescribable. Guru's power is indefinable. The accumulated merits of countless births results in getting the right guru."* Baba advised that practicing *Kriya* yoga by the women disciples having difficulty in conception related issues would make conceptions easier.

The learning of *Kriya* yoga, the essence of which has been given by Lord Krishna in Gita verses 4:29 and 5:27-28, is indeed the best thing that can happen to a spiritual aspirant. Arjuna queried in Gita verse 3:2 for a path that would definitely lead to the highest blessedness. Lord Krishna replied in Gita verse 3:3 that there are two paths: the path of knowledge and the path of meditative actions (right actions). *Babaji* gave the techniques of *Kriya* yoga to the world through Lahiri Mahasaya. The techniques came down to us through succession of *Kriya* yoga Masters.

We the *Kriyabans* (practitioner of Kriya yoga) got the right techniques to evolve ourselves to reach the immutable Self. It is us up to us, through our self-efforts, to make progress in that direction. Let us resolve to reach the Goal in this very incarnation.

Babaji Nagaraj

om kriya-babaji namaha om!—Salutation to *Kriya Babaji!*

Babaji Nagaraj, also known as *Kriya-Babaji* or just *Babaji* (dearly father), is not widely known. Those who have read the *Autobiography of a Yogi* by *Paramahamsa Yogananda*, know about *Babaji*. *Babaji* is the instrumental in reviving the *Kriya* Yoga tradition quoted in three Gita verses: 4.29, 5.27, and 5.28. These verses are quoted below:

Verse 4.29
> *apane juhvati pranam prane apanam tathapare*
> *pranapana-gati ruddhva pranayama-prayanah*

Translation: Other devotees offer as sacrifice the incoming breath of *prana* in the outgoing breath of *apana*, and the outgoing breath of *apana* in the incoming breath of *prana*, thus arresting the cause of inhalation and exhalation by intense practice of *pranayama*.

Verse 5.27 and 5.28
> *sparsan krtva bahir bahyams caksus caivantare bhruvoh*
> *pranapanau samau krtva nasabhyantara-carinau*
> *yatendriya-mano-budhir munir moksa-parayanah*
> *vigateccha-bhya-krodho yah sada mukta eva sah*

Translation: Shutting out all external sense objects, keeping the eyes and vision concentrated between the two eyebrows, suspending the inward and outward breaths within the nostrils, and thus controlling the mind, senses and intelligence, the muni (transcendentalist) aiming at liberation becomes free from desire, fear and anger. One who is always in this state is certainly liberated.

Arjuna in Gita verse 3.2 wants to know for certain the path that will lead to liberation. Lord Krishna answers in Gita verse 3.3, that only two paths: path of knowledge and path of meditative actions will lead to God realization. All other paths are secondary. Thus, revival of the *Kriya* Yoga tradition of Gita was the necessity and *Babaji* did it by initiating Lahiri Mahasaya in 1861. Lahiri Mahasaya had many disciples, who in turn had many disciples. Thus *Kriya* Yoga is now practiced worldwide. However, more to come! *Kriya* Yoga is predicted to be practiced more and more by many as the humanity progresses more and more towards spirituality. Thus, *Babaji* is a great reformer reviving the *Kriya Yoga* tradition of Gita. **This is a unique succession of *Kriya Yoga* gurus, since the original master *Babaji* is still living on the physical plane and making himself visible to a limited group of people, and inspiring them.** Yogananda has stated that *Babaji* is a *Maha Avatar* – great incarnation of the Godhead in the human form.

Babaji is a great master of yoga living today in the Himalayas. His body has not aged since the age of 16 when he conquered death and attained the supreme state of enlightenment. *Adi Sankaracharaya* in a poem describes Babaji his guru: "Behold under the banyan tree seated the aged disciples around their youthful teacher! This is strange indeed! The teacher instructs them only through silence, which is by itself sufficient to solve their doubts."

Since attaining *soruba samadhi* or physical immortality, Babaji has made it his mission to assist the suffering humanity in their quest for God realization. Usually, he has done so anonymously. Assistance has included prophets in the case of a few great souls – Sankar, Kabir, Lahiri Mahasaya, V.T. Neelakantan, and Yogi Ramaiah. *Babaji* himself has appeared and given them initiation: Sankar in the 8th century, Kabir in the 15th century, Lahiri Mahasaya in the 19th century, and Neelakantan and Ramaiah in the 20th century. Many more have seen *Babaji* in person.

Babaji told Lahiri Mahasaya and Ramaiah about initiating Sankaracharya (Sankar). Govindapada was Sankar's *shikhsa* guru and Babaji was Sankar's *diksha* guru.

After initiating, Babaji told Lahiri Mahasaya, "The *Kriya* yoga that I am giving to the world through you in this 19th century is the revival of the same *Kriya* science that Krishna gave millenniums ago to Arjuna, and that was later known to Patanjali and Christ, and to St. John, St. Paul and other disciples."

Kriya Yoga technique gives immediate and continuing positive results for the simultaneous development of the body, mind, intelligence, and soul. It is a simple psycho-physiological method by which human blood is de-carbonated and recharged with oxygen. The atoms of this extra oxygen are transmuted into life current to rejuvenate the brain and the spinal centers. The yogi is able to lessen or prevent decay of tissues.

The great guru has never openly appeared in any country; the misinterpreting glare of publicity has no place in his millennial plans. *Like the Creator, the sole but silent Power, Babji works in humble obscurity.*

Birth, living place, etc.

Babaji has revealed only a few details of his early years, only those which he believed to be formative as well as instructive to his disciples.

He was born on November 30, 203 AD (that is about 1800 years ago) in a small village now known as Parangipettai in Tamil Nadu near where Cauvery River flows into the Indian Ocean. The name Nagaraj was given to this child. Nagaraj means King of Serpents, to honor the great primordial force *"Kundalini Shakti"*. The child's birth coincided with the ascendancy of the star *Rohini*. It was the same star under which Lord Krishna was born.

Glimpses of his life – Jackfruit Incidence

Nagaraj's mother obtained a jackfruit when he was four years old. His mother set it aside for a family feast. It was a favorite fruit of the boy Nagaraj. During her absence from the house, Nagaraj seized the opportunity to devour the entire jackfruit mixed with honey with great relish. Upon her return, his mother seeing only the remains of the jackfruit, flew into a blind rage and stuffed a cloth down his mouth nearly suffocating him. Fortunately, Nagaraj survived. Nagaraj forgave his mother for nearly killing him. He thanked God for showing him that *she was to be loved without attachment or illusion*. His love for his mother became one of unconditional love and detachment.

Kidnapping Incidence

One day, five years old Nagaraj was standing to the left of the entrance gate of the Parangipettai Shiva temple compound. A foreigner suddenly seized him by the arm and carried him off. The kidnapper was a visiting trader from Baluchistan, now a part of Pakistan. He took Nagaraj in a sail boat northwards more than a thousand miles until they reached a port near what is now Kolkata (it is also mentioned Dhaka in a book). There, the kidnapper sold Nagaraj to a wealthy man as a slave. His owner was a kind man. He gave Nagaraj freedom shortly thereafter. As is often the case, what seemed to have been a great tragedy, actually set the stage for Nagaraj's liberation from the duties and limitations of a householder.

Nagaraj being freed, joined a small group of wandering monks (*sanyasins*). He was attracted by their radiant faces and love of God. Next few years, he wandered from place to place with the monks, and studied and learned various scriptures.

At age 11, he made a difficult trip from Benares with a group of ascetics to the sacred shrine of Katirgama in Sri Lanka at the southern most tip of the island. There he met Siddha (liberated person) Boganathar, and seeing his greatness Nagaraj became his disciple. Nagaraj performed intensive yogic practices for six months. Boganathar progressively initiated him into advanced techniques. Boganathar also inspired Nagaraja to seek initiation into *Kriya Kundalini Pranayama* from the legendary Siddha Agastyar at Courtrallam in the Pothigai Hills of Tamil Nadu, in what is now the Tinnevely District.

How hard do you have to try to get something you really want to have? Babaji advises until you can **tire your patience with patience.**

Babaji waited 48 days outside the ashram (hermitage) of Agastyar. On the 48th day when Babaji was on the verge of collapse, with great longing he simply repeated over and over again the name Agastyar. Agastyar suddenly came out and initiated Babji into the secrets *Kriya Kundalini pranayama* or *"Vasi Yogam"* as it is referred to in the writings of the Siddhas. Agastyar directed *Babaji* to go to Badrinath of the Himalayan Mountains and to become the greatest Siddha the world has ever known.

Babaji made the pilgrimage to Badrinath and then spent 18 "long and lonely months" practicing intensively all the yogic Kriyas taught to him by his gurus Agastyar and Boganathar. **After 18 months of arduous yogic discipline, Nagaraj entered a state of Soruba Samadhi wherein the Divinity descended, merged with and transformed the causal, subtle, and physical bodies. The physical body ceased to age and sparkled with a golden luster of divine incorruptibility. He was only 16 years at that time.** Sri Yukteshwar, the Guru of Yogananda, and who resurrected after his passing by his extraordinary yogic capabilities, said the yogic achievements of Babaji at the level of body cells were beyond imagination.

Presently, Babaji resides in an ashram near Badrinath. The ashram is known as Gauri Sankar Peetham. V. T. Neelakanthan of Madras whom Babaji met almost daily basis in 1952 and 1953 was allowed an astral visit (dream in physical body) in October 1953. The ashram is surrounded by sheer rock cliffs on all four sides with a row of caves at their base. The residents of the ashram numbered 14 at the time of the visit and the total number of immortals including Babaji were three. None can go within one mile of the ashram without Babaji's permission.

Bababji is very much up to date with the events in the world. In 1952-53, he mentioned about Narendra, Aurobindo, Shivananda, Swami Rama Tirtha, Indian independence, 10 Downing Street, the Statesman and other newspapers, America, modern living, etc. He knew about Anandamoyee Ma. Shivananda and Anandamoyee Ma were still living at that time. These showed Babaji's awareness of many things and everything that is going on in the world today and also that will be happening tomorrow.

Six main tenets of Babaji:

1. He is not for throwing away any worldly duties and responsibilities or for running away from home, family, and the world.
2. He is for living above worldliness, and he advises the strongest preparations before entering the world.
3. He attaches no special value whatsoever to one leaving the home and assuming sannyasin (monk) garb.
4. He does not suggest renouncing wealth, in the present age, Kali Yuga, barring rare exceptions, but suggests making the most righteous and benevolent use of it, remaining ever alert to avoid entanglement.
5. He is not for hating or evading women, but for developing the "motherliness eye".
6. His strongest emphasis is on living one's life (regardless of the circumstances of one's life) in a universal manner with love (prem) and service.

Above all, everyone should practice meditation and pranayama (controlled breathing) learning properly from a master.

Lahiri Mahasaya told his disciples that whoever remembers Babaji with devotion and love receives instant blessing from Babaji.

Please repeat with love and devotion: *Jai Babaji Jai* (glories to *Babaji*).

The Golden Key-Power of Scientific Prayer

By Emmet Fox

This article in this shorter form was taken from Studies in Truth Lessons (September 2008) published by Center for Spiritual Awareness (Director: Roy Eugene Davis).

Emmet Fox was one of the most influential New Thought teachers of the 20th Century. Born in 1886, from 1931 until he passed in 1951, he lectured weekly in New York City to thousands of truth seekers. *The Golden Key*, first published in a book and widely distributed as booklet, is an example of his simple, direct manner of teaching.

Scientific prayer will enable you to get yourself or anyone else out of any difficulty. It is the golden key to harmony and happiness. To those who have no acquaintance with the mightiest power in existence, this may appear to be a rash claim, but it needs only a fair trial to prove that, without a shadow of doubt, it is a just one. You need not take one's word for it, and you should not. Simply try it for yourself.

Beginners often get startling results the first time, for all that is essential is to have an open mind and sufficient faith to try the experiment. **Stop thinking about the difficulty, whatever it is, and start thinking about God instead. This is the complete truth, and if only you will do this, the trouble whatever it is will disappear.** It makes no difference what kind of trouble it is. Whatever it is, stop thinking about it and think of God instead—that is all you have to do.

But you must **stop thinking of the trouble,** whatever it is. The rule is, **to think about God**. To be continually glancing over your shoulder

58

in order to see how matters are progressing is fatal, because it is thinking of the trouble, and you must think of God and nothing else. Your object is to drive the thought of the difficulty out of your consciousness, **for a few moments at least,** substituting for it the thought of God. This is the crux of the whole thing. If you can become so absorbed in this consideration of the spiritual world that you forget for a while about the difficulty, you will find that you are safely and comfortably out of your difficulty.

In order to **"golden key"** a troublesome person or a difficult situation, think: "Now, I am going to 'golden key' John, or Mary, or that threatened danger": then proceed to drive all thought of John, or Mary, or the danger out of your mind, replacing it with the thought of God.

Do not try to think in advance what the solution to your difficulty will be. This is called "outlining" and will only delay the demonstration. Leave the question of ways and means to God. You want to get out of your difficulty; that is sufficient. You do your half, and God will never fail to do God's.

Jokes from Stephen Knapp (Stephen-knapp.com)

Collected by Haripada Dhar

IN RABBIT HEAVEN

Once there was a married couple who promised each other whoever died first would come back to tell the other what was heaven like. It happened to be that the husband died first. And sure enough, one evening the wife heard the voice of her husband, and she asked him, so what was it like.

He began to describe, "Well, first I get up in the morning and have an organic salad, then I have sex, then I eat again, then in the afternoon I have more sex. Then I have another meal of natural food, and again have more sex in the evening before I go to sleep."

The wife was quite surprised at this and asked, "So that is what it is like in heaven."

The husband replied, "Who said anything about heaven? I'm a bunny rabbit in Kansas."

SPINSTER SISTER

A man suffered a serious heart attack and had an open-heart bypass surgery. He awakened from the surgery to find himself in the care of nuns at a Catholic hospital. As he was recovering, a nun asked him questions regarding how he would like to pay for his treatment.

She asked if he had health insurance. He replied, in a raspy voice, "No health insurance."

The nun asked if he had money in the bank. He replied, "No money in the bank."

The nun asked, "Do you have a relative who could help you?" He said, "I only have a spinster sister, who is a nun."

The nun became agitated and announced loudly, "Nuns are not spinsters! Nuns are married to God."

The patient replied, "Well, then send the bill to my brother-in-law."

THERE IS NO CHAIR

An eccentric philosophy professor gave a one-question final exam after a semester dealing with a broad array of topics. The class was already seated and ready to go when the professor picked up his chair, plopped it on top of his desk and wrote on the board:

"Using everything we have learned this semester, prove that this chair does not exist."

Fingers flew, erasers erased, notebooks were filled in furious fashion. Some students wrote over 30 pages in one hour attempting to refute the existence of the chair. One member of the class however, was up and finished in less than a minute.

A week later when the grades were posted, the rest of the group wondered how he could have gotten an "A" when he had barely written anything at all.

His answer consisted of two words: "What chair?"

DOES GOD EXIST?

A man went to a barbershop to have his hair cut and his beard trimmed. As the barber began to work, they began to have a good conversation. They talked about so many things and various subjects.

When they eventually touched on the subject of God, the barber said: "I don't believe that God exists."

"Why do you say that?" asked the customer.

"Well, you just have to go out in the street to realize that God doesn't exist. Tell me, if God exists, would there be so many sick people? Would there be abandoned children? If God existed, there would be neither suffering nor pain. I can't imagine a loving a God who would allow all of these things."

The customer thought for a moment, but didn't respond because he didn't want to start an argument. The barber finished his job and the customer left the shop. Just after he left the barbershop, he saw a man in the street with long, stringy, dirty hair and an untrimmed beard. He looked dirty and unkempt.

The customer turned back and entered the barber shop again and he said to the barber: "You know what? Barbers do not exist."

"How can you say that?" asked the surprised barber. "I am here, and I am a barber. And I just worked on you!"

"No!" the customer exclaimed. "Barbers don't exist because if they did, there would be no people with dirty long hair and untrimmed beards, like that man outside."

"Ah, but barbers DO exist! What happens is, people do not come to me."

"Exactly!"- affirmed the customer. "That's the point! God, too, DOES exist! What happens, is, people don't go to Him and do not look for Him. That's why there's so much pain and suffering in the world."

Collection of Prayers

Ralph Waldo Emerson (1803-1882)

For each new morning with its light; for rest and shelter through the night; for health and food; for love and friends; for everything Thy goodness sends.

Saint Francis of Assisi (1181-1226)

Lord, make me an instrument of Thy peace. Where there is hatred, let me sow love; where there is injury, pardon; where there is error, truth; where there is discord, harmony; where there is doubt, faith; where there is despair, hope; where there is darkness, light; and where there is sorrow, joy.

Oh Divine Master, grant that I may not so much seek to be consoled, as to console; to be understood, as to understand; to be loved, as to love. For it is in giving that we receive; it is pardoning that we are pardoned; and it is in dying [to self-centeredness] that we are born to eternal life.

From *Paramahamsa* Yoganandaji

Day and night, day and night
You are with me day and night
Will my days pass away?
Without realizing You, O my Lord!
From Joy I have come. In Joy I live, move, and have my being. And in that sacred Joy I will melt again.

From Ellen Grace O'Brian (*A Single Blade of Grass*)

Prayer for the workplace: "God, be my planner today. Help me to remember that You call all the meetings and that all work is done for Your sake. When I see my coworkers, I will think only of You, offering my service to You."

Prayer before Meals

Gita Verse 4-24

Brahmarpanam brahma havir brahmagnau brahmana hutam

brahmaiva tena gantavyam brahmakarmasamadhina

Whatever we offer is Brahman, the clarified butter (ghee) to be offered into the fire is Brahman, whoever offers is Brahman Himself. He will ultimately go to the Brahman after completing his duties, Brahman in action.

Gita Verse 15-14

Aham vaisvanara bhutva praninam deham asritah
prapanasamayukta pacami annam caturvidham

Having become the digestive fire, it is I who abide in all living beings, and having been united with the life forces Prana and Apana, it is I who digest the four kinds of foods.

Gita Verse 9-27

Yat karosi yad asnasi yaj juhosi dadasi yat
yat tapasyasi kaunteya tat kurusva madarpanam

Whatever you do, whatever you eat, whatever you offer as an oblation, whatever you give, and whatever austerity you practice, do that as an offering to me.

4.th Verse of Meal time Prayer

Hari data Hari bhokta
Hari annam prajapati
Hari sarva sarireshu,
bhungte bhojaete Hari

Lord Hari is the giver and enjoyer; He is the food we eat. He resides in everybody. He eats, and feeds everyone.

Four Small Heart-Touching Incidents

In the later part of stay in our house at 404 Princeton Circle in College Station, TX, USA, the first two incidents occurred. We stayed at this house for about 15 years and moved out first week of January in 2007. The third incident occurred outside of the front door of my laboratory (BCS Fuel Cells, Inc.) at 2812 Finfeather Road in Bryan, TX, USA, during the time period 2006-2007.

A Baby Bird

In one incidence, in one afternoon, I was standing outside in our backyard. I noticed a small baby mocking (perhaps) bird sitting on the roof and the mother bird sitting on an electrical pole at the end of our yard. As I was looking carefully at the baby bird I felt a strong telepathic message that he was looking for some food.

This was a spring season and was the regular breeding season for birds. All birds are busy eating, building nest, mating, laying eggs, hatching their eggs, and taking care of the baby birds. When the baby bird is about to fly out of the nest, I believe the baby bird has a good meal from the mother, fly out from the nest and can take care of himself with some help from his mother. Some baby birds may have their tummies empty or insufficient food and cannot take care of themselves to fly out or finding some food. In some cases, the mother bird cannot or does not have the capability of taking sufficient care of her baby at that time. In those cases the baby birds are on their own to take care of themselves and can succumb to their helplessness.

It was one of those occasions that I happened to notice the baby bird on top of our roof and I felt that he was looking for food. I went inside the house and brought some mixture of seeds sold in super markets as "bird seeds" in my hand. We had always some stock of bird food in our house as we regularly fed birds in a bird feeder. As soon as the baby bird saw the food in my hand, he flew right on me on my shoulder and I sat down on the grass to make him sit comfortably on my knee and he immediately made himself comfortable on one of my knees. Seeing this, my wife came out from the house and assisted me in the feeding process. The bird seeds consisted of a mixture various kinds of grain seeds and sunflower seeds. He showed interest only on the sunflower seeds. But then we realized that we had to peel the seeds opened which we did and fed him as he opened his mouth. He was very hungry and we fed him probably about five minutes. He ate and ate until he did not want to eat any more. We gave one or two drops of water in his mouth and made him sit alone under the shade of our open porch. The mother bird was watching all along sitting on the top of a telephone pole. Our cat named Mickey was watching us through the window and wanted eagerly to come out. Obviously, we did not let the cat come outside to disturb the baby bird.

The baby bird rested about 5 minutes under the shade of our porch. The mother bird flew one or two times over the baby bird still sitting on the shaded porch. The baby bird then finding sufficient strength flew away to a nearby small tree.

I felt myself as an agent of God to be able to help the baby bird. I thanked God for making me available for this small help that my wife and I were able to render to this bird.

A Lame Craw Fish

One afternoon at the end of my daily office routine I came home. My wife told me that she saw a craw fish crawling to our backyard from the small and somewhat polluted creek which runs through our property marking the boundary of our backyard. Immediately we went outside and spotted the craw fish entering our drive-in area. It was about 3-4 inches long and it had one front-leg missing. It was crawling and crawling and apparently was looking for a safe haven to go to. I went inside and found out a rectangular container, put some water in it, and brought it out. I picked up the craw fish and put him in the container. The craw fish immediately felt comfortable and was enjoying the water. What to do with the craw fish? A thought came in that we should take him to a larger water source and let him out there. After a few mental searches, we thought about the large pond in the property of the Central Park of the City of College Station, our home town. This pond is about two miles from our home. I drove the lame craw fish in the container to the pond and let him go into the water. As he felt the water of the pond he gradually submerged himself. I felt he was very comfortable and happy to enter into the water and disappeared slowly into the depth of the pond. I thanked God very much for helping this craw fish finding home after his long surviving struggle. I was just an instrument in God's hands to be able to render the services to this craw fish.

A Thirsty Baby Bird

I used to take lunch from my home to my office. After I had my lunch, one day I went out for a short period closing the front door (the back door is always closed normally). When I came back I noticed at the entrance and a few inches to the right a small bird sitting and opening his mouth upward. It was a sparrow and seemed bigger for a sparrow, and probably because it was young and fluffy. It appeared to me like a statue, sitting there not blocking the door. It could be easily unnoticed and camouflaged with the door, and the wall and the walkway in front of our office unit, and perhaps escaped the notice of others while it was sitting there until I came to notice it.

Initially, I thought it was someone's trick placing a bird's figurine in front our door. As I tried to pick it up, it moved slightly telling me that it was a live bird needing immediate help. I had some cookies that I keep for snacks. Leaving the bird where it was, I immediately brought some crumbs of cookies and tried to put small amounts into his still-open mouth and he still sitting outside. However the bird did not show any interest in feeding. Next, my thought was to give him some water. In a small clean beaker, I brought out some distilled water that we keep for our laboratory. I poured a very little amount into his mouth. He immediately swallowed the water. I repeated this process of feeding water a few more times. He swallowed water each time and closed his beaks. I tried to give him some more cookie crumbs, but it did not show any interest in this food. After the drink, he took rest for a minute and flew to the top of the roof where a few more sparrows were sitting.

I thanked God for making me an agent for rendering His help to this bird in need.

A Hungry Cat

It was some years ago, when I used to attend regularly Sunday activities in our temple at Highway 6 near Navasota. One cat was meowing going from one door to another door of the two buildings of our temple. At the time of the incident there were two buildings: one the main temple and the other a small mobile home that housed some classes for children. That cat meowed very urgently and would try to come in, but no one would let him in. It continued almost the entire period of the temple was open in the morning. At the end of the *aarathi* (prayer with light and incense) ceremony, *prasadam* (sanctified food) was distributed. I came out with *prasadam* in my hand, and the cat was there at the door. I gave him the sanctified food consisting of banana pieces and some sweets. He ate very quickly. Generally, a cat would not eat these kinds of food. As he was very hungry, he ate and was still hungry.

I narrated the story to my family. In the afternoon I came to temple with my daughter Monisha to look for the cat and brought some cat-food with us (we used to have a pet cat). As I parked the car in the parking lot, the cat came again near us meowing and walking a quite a bit distance probably one-eighth of a mile. We gave the food to the cat. He ate very hurriedly showing his hunger again. We brought the cat home and took care of for the night. Following day, I took him to the animal shelter, and left him there with a small donation for his food and shelter. Thank you God for taking care of this hungry cat!

Nine Planets

Navagrahas (nine planets) in the Vedic tradition

Before I begin my talk, I would like to take a minute or two telling few words accepting the position of Vice President of the Temple Committee. I sincerely thank Srinivasa and Jayakumar for requesting me to accept this position. And I agreed to help Srinivasa, our President, in any way I can.

As you know the temple came into existence some years ago. The temple has been a real boon to all of us. You know God's cosmic Laws of Cause and Effect, also known as the Laws of Karma. The building the temple was possible because of past good Karma of all of us as a community. The temple has provided so much opportunity for all to grow spiritually, for volunteering work, selfless work, and to become a close-knit community in this area. I urge you all to participate in temple programs and activities.

It was customary to chant the hymns on *Navagrahas* during the celebration of Makar Sankranti. Nava means "nine" and the *graha* can be translated into planet. *Navagrahas* literally means "nine planets." The exact usage of the words *graha* and planet are different as noted below in this article. Makar Sankranti marks the beginning of the harvest season in India. Sankranti means transmigration of the Sun from one *Rashi* to another. Makar Sankranti (which falls on January 14) marks the beginning of the northern movement of the Sun (also known as *Uttarayan*) as a sign of the approaching summer season. The period July 14 to January 14 is known as *Dakshinayan* marking the movement of the Sun towards the South as a sign of the approaching winter season.

One thought that can come to an inquisitive mind during chanting of the hymns of the *Navagrahas*, or during worshiping of the deities representing

70

them to ward off any inauspicious possibilities coming onto him is: are these *Navagrahas* the same as the sun's nine planets we know of?

Every educated person is familiar with the nine planets referred to above of the solar system. They are Mercury, Venus, Earth, Mars, Jupiter, Saturn, Uranus, Neptune, and Pluto. These planets are different from the *navagrahas* of the Vedic tradition. It is a mere coincidence that in both cases the number is nine. In fact, in 2006, the sun's planet Pluto had been officially denigrated not to be considered a planet, but similar to innumerable objects that are known to rotate around the sun. There are now eight recognized planets of the sun, and three dwarf planets, Ceres, Pluto, and Eris.

But the number of *grahas* is still nine effecting lives on the earth. These nine grahas form the foundation of the Vedic astrology.

Naturally, it comes to our minds if the planets of the solar system that we know can be reconciled with nine *grahas* of the Vedic tradition. The term *"graha"* in Sanskrit language has been translated into English as *"planet"*. English is comparatively a newer language compared to Sanskrit. A planet is a celestial body orbiting a star that is massive enough to be rounded by its own gravity. A cause for confusion can arise if the term *graha* is translated as to mean a planet with reference to understanding the *Navagrahas* of the Vedic tradition.

The term "graha" means any celestial body that has the power to control or grasp specially signifying influencing life on the planet Earth. Thus the term *graha* of the Vedic age includes the Sun, which is not a planet in the modern sense of the term, but is a star, the originator of planets.

I wanted to clarify the difference between the *navagrahas* and the nine traditional planets of the solar system. Even though the number nine comes in both cases, does it mean the nine planets as we know belonging to the solar system are the same as mentioned in Vedic scriptures? This is a natural question that comes when we recite the verses of hymns on *Navagrahas*. Actually, they are not the same. As mentioned above, the term *graha* has a different usage. These *navagrahas* are the following: **Sun, Mercury, Venus, Moon, Rahu, Ketu, Mars, Jupiter, and Saturn**.

Earth is a planet (graha), but it is not included in the list since the influence of the *Navagrahas* refers to the people on earth. Sun is a *graha* and is a star (not a planet). Moon is a *graha*, and a natural satellite of the Earth. The *grahas*, Rahu and Ketu, do not have any physical masses but merely are points in the space having attraction or influence on the people on earth. If we think a little bit carefully on the introduction of Rahu and Ketu, one cannot but be amazed that our ancient seers and the astrologers in the Vedic period came up with the existence of these two imaginary points in space that have influence on the people on earth in determining their future evolution.

Astrology studies the effect of the nearby celestial bodies and their relative positions in understanding, interpreting, and organizing information about human personality, human affairs and other terrestrial matters. In the Vedic tradition, such celestial bodies included the Sun, Moon, and sun's planets, such as Mercury, Venus, Mars, Jupiter, and Saturn. All these have physical masses. Two shadowy *grahas* had been found to have also influence on terrestrial life and matters similar to the *grahas* having physical masses. These two shadowy *grahas* are Rahu and Ketu.

Let us try to understand the origin of Rahu and Ketu with reference to two figures. Figure 1 shows the earth's yearly orbit around the sun. It is also known as the solar ecliptic to an observer on the earth. It is the apparent path in the celestial sphere, the sun is seen to move yearly basis. Also shown in Fig. 1 is the moon's orbit around the earth. This orbit makes about 5° angle with the earth's orbit around the sun. Thus moon spends most of the time above or below the earth's orbit. No eclipses can occur under these conditions. Two to four times each year, the moon passes through a portion of the earth's penumbral or umbral shadows near the lunar nodes, and causing an eclipse to occur.

A larger perspective view of the depiction in Fig. 1 is given in Fig. 2 as it would appear to an observer on the earth. The sun appears to move along the solar ecliptic and the moon along the lunar ecliptic. The two paths cross at the two nodes, known in Vedic astrology as Rahu and Ketu The sun's path makes a complete revolution in one year. The moon's circular path is completed in about one month. Every month moon overtakes the sun, which appears to move slowly. Usually, the moon's path passes above or below the sun's path. Periodically, the moon overtakes the sun near the place where their paths intersect. This causes sun or the moon to be hidden from the earth's view, and the result is a solar or a lunar eclipse. The places of intersection are the north and south lunar nodes, also called Rahu and Ketu in Hindu mythology or in Vedic astrology. In the language of the mythology, the Rahu and Ketu are said to "swallow up" the sun and the moon. Even though it is not literally so, but figuratively it means that Rahu and Ketu are responsible for causing the eclipses, and this is true. Rahu and Ketu symbolically eclipse the sun and the moon. Sun represents consciousness and the moon represents the mind. Rahu and Ketu have been given the status of *grahas* to emphasize their significance and importance in the Vedic astrology. These two planets have no substance, but they have enormous importance and significance in dealing with death, re-birth, transformation and regeneration of lives on earth.

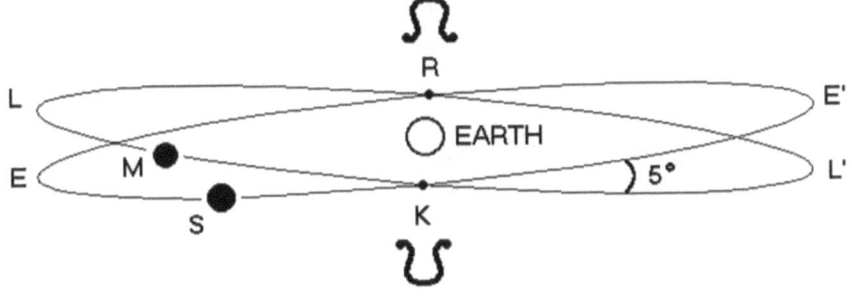

Figure 1

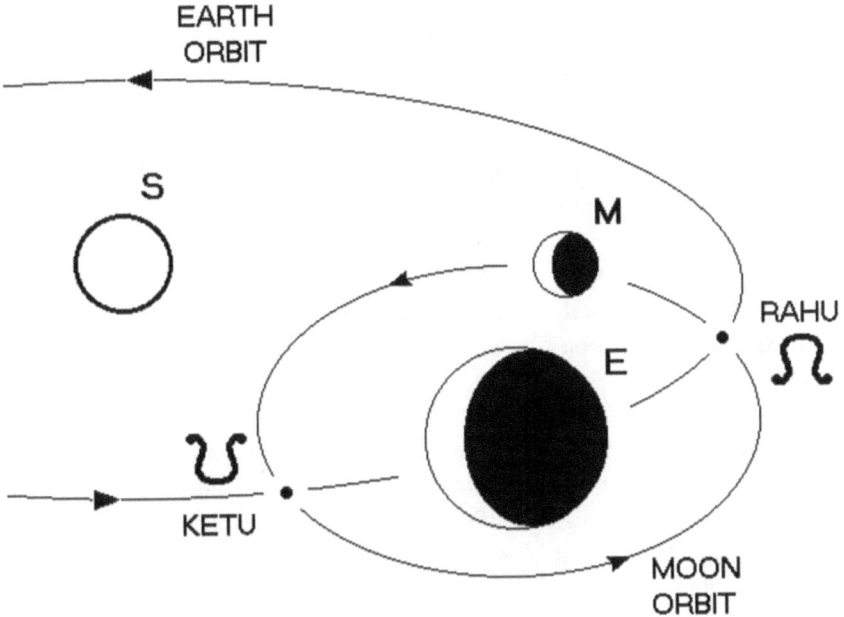

Figure 2

Swami Rama Tirtha

Swami Rama Tirtha is said to be a direct descendent of Gossain Tulsi Das, the immortal author of the widely read Hindi Ramayana. He was born in 1873 at Muraliwala in the province of Punjab in undivided India. He was previously known as Gosain Tirtha Rama. His mother passed away when he was only a few days old, and he was brought up by his elder brother, Gossain Gurudas.

As a child Rama was very fond of listening to recitations from the Holy Scriptures and attending Kathas. He often put questions to holy men and even offered explanations.

Rama was only ten years old when his father got him married. His father left him under the care of his friend Bhakta Dhana Rama, a man of great purity and simplicity of life. Rama regarded him Guru. His surrender to his Guru was so complete that he never did anything without first consulting him.

Rama was a brilliant student, especially in mathematics. He topped the list in B.A. and took his M.A. degree in mathematics. For two years Rama was a professor of mathematics in a Lahore College.

He and his wife had two sons. When he was teaching in the college, his spiritual life began to blossom. He began to read Gita and became a great devotee of Lord Krishna.

A great impetus was given to his spiritual life by Swami Vivekananda, whom he saw for the first time at Lahore. The sight of the great Swami as Sannyasin kindled in him the longing to don the ochre robe.

In the year 1900, Rama Tirtha went to the forest and soon became a Sannyasin. His wife, two children and few others accompanied him to the Himalayas. Owing to ill health, his wife later returned with one of her sons. The other was left at Tehri for his schooling there.

During the years 1902 and 1904, Rama visited Japan and the United States. He thrilled the Japanese with his inspiring and soul-elevating speeches. He spent about a year and a half in San Francisco under the hospitality of Dr. Albert Hiller. He gained a large following and started many societies, one of them being the Hermetic Brotherhood, dedicated to the study of Vedanta. His charming personality had a great impact on the Americans. Devout Americans looked upon him as the living Christ.

On his return to India, Swami Rama continued to lecture in the plains, but his health began to break down. He went back to the Himalayas and settled at the Vasistha Ashram.

One day in October 1906, while bathing in the Ganges near Tekri Garwal, Swamiji was accidentally drowned. He was only 33 years old. He wrote just before his death:

"Oh death, take away this body if you will. I have many more bodies to live with. I can afford to live happily in the silver threads of the moon and the golden rays of the sun. I shall roam free singing the guise of hilly brooks and streams. I shall be dancing happily in the waves of the sea. I am the graceful gait of the breeze and the wind inebriated. Those forms of mine are wandering forms of change. I came down from the tops, knocked at doors, awakened the sleeping, consoled one, wiped the tears of another, covered some, and took of the veils of others. I doff my hat and off I am. I keep nothing with me. Nobody can find me."

It is clear that what seemed to be an accident was not an accident at all, but the Swami intentionally wanted to leave his body this way.

Swami Rama's works has been published in a seven-volume compilation called "In the Woods of God-Realization."

Rama Tirtha was a great ascetic and an enlightened mystic. He practiced yoga on the banks of the river Ravi. Later he lived in the forests of Brahmapuri, on the banks of the river Ganges, five miles away from Rishikesh, and attained Self-Realization.

He was bashful like a modest girl. Living as he did in the light of love, he looked transparently pure through his small, frail, fair-colored body. But under this unassuming humble appearance there lay hidden a remarkable man with some lofty aspirations and noble aims.

From out of a thin and frail body, he managed to emerge a strong man of stag-like nimble activity. He was a great and swift walker. He could walk more than forty miles a day as a Swami in the Himalayan Hills. He won a 40 mile race, in America, which he ran for fun with American soldiers. He came two hours ahead of them.

He scaled Gangotri, Jamunotri, and Badrinath peaks in a small strip of loin cloth and blanket. He crossed through glaciers from Jumunotri to

Gangotri. He lived in snows and slept in caves in thick dreary jungles all alone. The mountain people hallowed the Swami as a Deva so strong that he would ferry their cattle from the opposite bank to their village across a swift hill torrent in the rainy season. At midnight, he would leave his abode go about roaming in the dark jungles defying fear and death. He was so fearless, so bold, so vehement, so strong, and so cheerful.

His face became full, beautifully tinted and his eyes half-closed with divine intoxication. With all his exuberance of physical and spiritual energy, Swami RT presented to the world the masterpiece of his life work, namely, his own personality

Swamiji's personality may well be described as explosive. He would remain silent for months long, as if he had nothing to say. He remained merged in joy. Then suddenly, he would burst like a volcano and out would come his thoughts, spoken in a wild manner. Whenever he spoke or wrote, it would be something very refreshing and original. It seems he could not remain long in the society without feeling some kind of loss, which entailed weariness of soul to him. He would attribute all his ailments to the "business talks" of men of worldly wisdom, who at times gathered around him. He protested against all advice of worldly wisdom.

Swamiji was a man of tears. In the middle of the discourses, he would enter into the spirit of his sayings and become silent for minutes with tears trickling down from his closed eyes. Such an attitude led the whole of the audience into the spirit of his thoughts. He was wonderful creature, who at the climax of his oration would sleep in the Divine, and also lull his audience into slumber. When he awoke, his eloquence, it seems, would end in shrieks and cries.

Krishna Vision

In the early days, he seldom spoke in public without shedding tears at the very name of Sri Krishna. He beheld Him on the Kadamba tree heard his flute ringing in his ears, while bathing in the Ganges at Haridwar. In house at Lahore, he read "Sur Sagar" with glorious passion that brought him the vision of Krishna, after which he swooned away. That very day after the swoon, he saw a serpent with upturned hood in his room, and beheld Sri Krishna dancing on his hood. It is stated that for days and nights he wept in love of Lord Krishna.

He was always merry like birds. Never a frown or a scowl darkened his eyebrows. Men would come and Swamiji would greet them with nothing, but peal after peal of ringing laughter and what would happen?

They immediately bow down to him, confess their inmost guilt, and seek protection from sin and darkness.

In the midst of laughter, he would suddenly become mute, shut his eyes, and begin to chant in the most solemn tunes the sacred syllable AUM. He used to say, "I am a storm of peace. I am a tempest of joy."

He used to say that he believed in experimental religion. Theology has little or nothing whatsoever to do with the inner religion of the living man. Just as in science authority has little weight in arriving at the truth, so in religion authority should have little or no weight. Man's own inner experience are the final test of truth. Everyone must go to God through failures and successes of his own life.

Western Hinduism

The following comments were sent to the editor of *Hinduism Today* in response to an article published in the October-December (2005) issue of the magazine.

Swami Shankarananda's article, Confessions of a Western Hindu, has brought out a very important issue for many individuals and groups practicing Hinduism in essence but not calling themselves Hindus. Swamiji has given good reasons that should help these people that it is acceptable to be known as Hindus despite some hesitations and points against it. It is the start of an evolution of Hinduism in another setting outside India. If you are a follower of the traditions represented by Hinduism, it is all right to be called a Hindu, maybe with some qualification, like, a Western Hindu.

Hinduism is a relatively recent term. It denotes what had been known throughout the ages as the *Sanatan Dharma* (eternal religion). Perhaps, to be called a follower of *Sanatan Dharma* would be more appealing. But then *Sanatan Dharma* is Hinduism. The followers of the Bhagavad Gita and the Vedas, believers in *Karma* and reincarnation, worshippers of deities with belief in one ultimate reality, practitioners of yoga and meditation, followers of the Hindu tradition and spirituality, should mean to be Hindus, whatever name be given to them. If the person is hesitant to be identified with Hinduism, and if the person is comfortable with other identifications, like, Western, American, European, or Asian Hinduism to distinguish it from the main stream Indian or Eastern Hindu tradition, it should be all right and acceptable.

I fully understand the points raised by Swamiji for shying away for the followers of the Hindu tradition for not calling themselves Hindu in the western countries and elsewhere outside India (and Nepal). To a newcomer in Hinduism, aside from the wealth of spirituality and philosophical knowledge, Hinduism brings connotations of historical societal imperfections which had occurred and remnants of which still exist (for example, in the form of caste system). But, only in Hinduism are there so many holy men and women filled with mysticism and on the path of God that none else can match. Only the realization of the Self and God can bring true happiness, and nothing else.

The first generation Hindus in the West will see a gradual dilution of their culture they bring along with them. The subsequent generations of Hindus will face similar situation faced by the new Western Hindus: difficult to identify with the mainstream Hinduism. The emergence of Hinduism in the form of Western Hinduism, for example, should help the new generation of Hindus of Indian origin in the West for them to accept and identify themselves with.

A person accepting the part Hindu culture, such as, yoga or meditation, may or may not identify with the Hinduism, but a person totally accepting the Hindu tradition, should identify with the Hinduism. Identifying themselves by different name should not be the correct way of doing it. If a person follows the Hindu tradition, he should find a comfortable name for it as suggested above. Following the Hindu tradition and to deny it outright would not be correct. It is not proper to give the tradition a new name, since it is an Eternal Way of living. Give the name, which already exists. Modify it if comfortable by adding prefixes Western, European, etc.

Letter of Congratulations

The following letter (dated May 26, 2009) was received unsolicited from my supervisor and mentor at Texas A&M University, Professor John O'M. Bockris, a famous electrochemist of his time.

Dear Hari,

Thank you very much for contributing a fine paper to my celebratory volume. I think that of the many electrochemists I have known you have been one out of perhaps three who have really shown that you could make it, i.e., that you could come out into the struggle which is public life in the USA and come out on top.

Once more congratulations!

However, before I close this short note, I want to point out what you probably already realize that the fuel cell business goes up and down, but probably it's in a period of down owing to the fact that everyone concludes that fuel cells are too expensive. They also apply to hydrogen fuel, not because when comes out of the reactor which it makes it, it is expensive, but because it becomes more expensive on the way to the consumer (it has to be stored, perhaps taken to a low temperature, sent to the consumer) but the worst thing is that it has to be reconverted to electricity. I want to suggest to you therefore for your earnest consideration that may be you should turn your thoughts a little toward bio fuel cells. You probably would not be in disagreement with me if I said, in my opinion, the electricity of the body comes from a myriad of fuel cells in biological organisms. I think that the electrodes of the bio fuel cells are the enzymes which are absorbed upon the surface of the fuel cell and I think it's fairly easy to make models showing always two enzymes connected with biological action.

It has puzzled biochemists for many years that find that some reactions in the body act against the free energy gradient, but this is not difficult to understand if you have fuel cells to give the energy demanded. Of course, we have this in the simplest example in water electrolysis, which is electricity overcoming free energy.

Anyway, it's not too likely that I shall see you now and I very much want to congratulate you on your achievements and hope that they continue.

Yours Sincerely,
John O'M. Bockris

A reply to the above letter was as follows:

Dear Dr. Bockris,

We are very pleased that you liked our article in the J. Solid State Electrochemistry in celebration of your birthday.

I appreciate very much your kind remarks about me and my activities in the practical aspects of fuel cell research and development in my company. I am touched very much. In our philosophy it is stated that everything happens through the good wishes of the masters (teachers, mentors) along with the grace from the heavenly Lord. I very much thank you and my other mentors for whatever I have been able to achieve.

I appreciate very much your suggestion of bio-fuel cells as an area to get into. I would definitely look into the prospect of initiating this area. I have the book, Modern Aspects of Bio-electrochemistry, edited by Dr. Felix Gutmann. This book should provide enough materials for background reading.

With my best regards and my prayers for your good health,
Haripada Dhar

The Liberation War as it Felt
to a Bangladeshi Student
in Ottawa, Canada

I came to Canada from East Pakistan at the end of 1967 to attend St. Francis Xavier University at Antigonish, Nova Scotia. I completed my Master's degree there in 1969 studying under the guidance of Dr. E. A. Secco. I was admitted to University of Ottawa in the Department of Chemistry 1969 in the Ph.D. program of studies under the direction of Dr. Brian E. Conway. I finished my Ph.D. degree at the end of 1973. The intense civil war or the liberation war for independent Bangladesh continued during the period 1970-71. Thus, I was in a position to view the events of the civil war from being outside the country. In this article, I have made an attempt to describe some of the events and my feelings at that time.

It was my dream trip to a foreign advanced country for higher education. It brought me to tears many times whenever the thought came to my mind where I was and what I was doing. Coming from a very humble background in that troubled country (Bangladesh), I was not able to contain these emotions.

In Ottawa, I started my Ph.D. program. After the civil war started in Bangladesh, and hearing about so much trouble and death, I was very thankful to the Lord for letting me out of the country. Otherwise, I would have faced certain death, or trouble indescribable. The Lord took me out of the region before I was trapped inside the military armors and certainly face untimely death. More importantly being outside the troubled country, I was in a position to help my family and others. I thanked the Lord that I got admitted and thanked the authorities of the then East Pakistan government for issuing me a passport and letting me get out of the country as a student.

Many aspiring students were not so lucky during the liberation war time. Many were not allowed to leave even with a valid passport. One such student was Mr. Amalendu Chatterjee. He was a graduate from Bangladesh University of Engineering and Technology. I came to know him from the beginning of his stay in Ottawa. He was admitted to the Electrical Engineering Department at the University of Ottawa. The then Pakistani government would not allow him to leave even though he got admission for higher education abroad. In 1972, Amalendu contacted the EE Department again from a refugee camp in India. The Department was very sympathetic to his cause. Dr. Ahmed, and a few staff members of the department played a very active role to provide moral support. I came to know from Dr. Ahmed about Amalendu's admission in the graduate program in the fall session of 1971. Due to some political reasons, he could only come in the 1972 fall session after Bangladesh was established as a sovereign nation. I was one of the few persons to receive Amalendu in the university campus. He finished his M.S. and Ph.D. programs. It was great a pleasure to see him succeed in life. Later, I came to know one touching story of his life. In the period of nine-month ordeal during the liberation movement, Amalendu did not know if his parents were alive and his parents did not know if Amalendu was alive. It was a very emotional gathering when they met each other in their home at the island of Sandwip in Bangladesh, after Amalendu traveled from Kolkata to Bangladesh at the end of December 1971.

We would like Bangladesh to be a secular Muslim country and thus set an example to the world. Secularism will increase national pride, strength, and stability; and honor and respect from other nations.

I heard and dealt with much painful and sad news at the personal level from my embattled country East Pakistan on the way to be free Bangladesh: My family's leaving the country as the military entered our village, Araihazar. Members of the minority faith, in particular, the Hindus were the target of attack because of the support by India of the liberation army and the presumption that Hindus are pro-Indian. Under attack the Hindus usually took shelters in the houses of their Muslim friends. A number of people and have been caught and killed in our village. Jagannath Hall, a university residence for the minority students under Dhaka University was searched and attacked by the military. I resided at this hall for five years while I was a student at the Dhaka University long time ago in the period 1961-1965. Many students from J. N. Hall were killed military style using gun fires in the foreground of the hall. The sad event was video-taped by someone not far from the hall area. Dr. Govinda Chandra Deb, the Provost of the hall, a professor in the Department of Philosophy was killed in his residence. Dr. Deb, a philosopher and a humanist was a life-long bachelor. Also killed were Dr. Santosh Bhattacharjee (History professor) and Jyotirmoy Guha-Thakuratha (English professor). The latter two were House Tutors at the Hall. I knew all of them at the personal level.

The military went village to village, city to city, plundering, committing atrocities against the people. Hearing that the military had arrived in our village, my family members, leaving all possessions behind, started moving towards the Indian border of the state of Tripura. Traveling via the Indian state of Assam, my family members came to the state of West Bengal for shelter. I know at least two persons in our village who were caught by the military and shot dead. It is to be mentioned here that most people from Bangladesh arriving in India face very uncertain future. Those, who come without documentation, do not get recognition from the Indian government. These people cannot get any job. They become easy prey to adversity and death. I know few people migrating to India died at younger ages.

During the period of the liberation war, there were no good media for communications with the family members. I heard the news of our family's fleeing the troubled region when they arrived and semi-settled in West Bengal. There were no emails in those days, and there were no telephone connections from villages. Frequent telephone contacts were uncommon in those days. We depended on the sometimes unreliable postal services. I wrote every week or every two weeks to let my well-wishers know I was are all right.

It was certainly the beginning of the age of long distance live TV telecasting. 1969 saw the moon-landing through TV. Evening news and nightly news brought news from India, Pakistan, and other countries of the world. We would watch CBC nightly news with Lloyd Robertson at 11 PM before going to bed for the night. Another TV personality was Stanley Burke who was openly known to support the causes of the separation of East Pakistan seeing the atrocities committed by the Pakistan military in that region.

There were meetings to discuss ways to help people in need in Bangladesh. Perhaps thousands of dollars were raised and sent through the International Red Cross organization. There was an overwhelming support of all Bangladeshis and Indians (except perhaps very few I imagine) living there in Ottawa.

One day, my professor Dr. Conway invited me for lunch to discuss the events of Bangladesh fighting. Dr. Conway himself being of British origin took particular interest in the events. That I am from that troubled region interested him little bit more. He asked me how much money I needed to send my displaced family now in India. I estimated at that time, it was being about one thousand dollars. However, he did not offer any additional financial assistance for that cause; maybe it was too personal.

I recall at least one demonstration staged by the sympathizers against war in East Pakistan which I participated. It was in the Parliament Hill. It was a peaceful demonstration with placards waving by the participants. I think there was a meeting inside after the demonstration with a government official.

Canadian government and the public in general were sympathetic towards the Bengalis for their causes. Canadian government was the second country next to India to recognize independent Bangladesh. Newspapers in general were also sympathetic towards the causes of the Bengalis. I remember one editor in a daily newspaper in Ottawa, who was from West Pakistan, was sympathetic towards the causes of the Pakistani Government. In his editorials, he was always anti-Bengalis. One fellow student I knew from West Pakistan. He was strongly for the Pakistani Government. He said the government was not doing enough to crush the Bengalis.

Sheikh Mujibur Rahaman visited Ottawa in 1973 to attend the Commonwealth Conference as the Head of the independent Bangladesh. There was a gathering in a hotel at Ridau Street in Ottawa. I attended the gathering. He gave a speech in Bengali, triumphant over Yahya Khan.

I love my motherland, Bangladesh, and wish her all well; and also I wish happiness for all people who live there.

Short Biography of Haripada Dhar

Dr. Dhar received his Ph.D. degree in Chemistry specializing in Electrochemistry from the University of Ottawa, Canada, under the guidance of Dr. Brian E. Conway, a prominent electrochemist. His Ph.D. thesis work dealt with investigations on the studies of electrical double layer. Earlier, he received his Master's degree from Saint Francis Xavier University, Antigonish, Nova Scotia, Canada.

Dr. Dhar is the President of BCS Fuel Cells, Inc. He has established himself as a leader in the PEM (proton exchange membrane) fuel cell industry offering simplified and easy-to-operate fuel cells and systems. Dr. Dhar is an electrochemist having both academic and industrial experiences. He has a strong background in work related to fuel cell development. He has carried out half-cell measurements related to hydrogen oxidation and oxygen reduction on gas diffusion electrodes. He carried out detailed investigations on the extent of catalyst poisoning by CO (carbon monoxide) present in hydrogen fuels. He has carried out optimization studies on the development of high power density fuel cells, and regenerative fuel cells. He is one of the early leaders in the development of self-humidified fuel cells, including designing and building PEM fuel cell stacks and systems. The work in the PEM fuel cell area has led to the issuance of 4 US patents. Dr. Dhar has introduced about 15 models of stacks and systems for sale and has sold about 500 fuel cell stacks and systems. He has 45 publications, including 5 patents and 2 book articles.

He received unsolicited letters of appreciations from customers around the world using his fuel cell products: membrane-electrodes assemblies and fuel cell stacks of various capacities. He received an unsolicited letter of congratulations (appreciations) from the eminent electrochemist Dr. John O'M. Bockris, who was his supervisor and mentor at Texas A&M

University. Dr. Bockris was an advocate for the use of clean fuel hydrogen related to fuel cell operations.

He is an initiate in the *Kriya Yoga* meditation in the lineage of *Babaji*, learning the technique from yoga masters, Roy Eugene Davis of the Center for Spiritual Awareness and from *Paramahamsa Hariharananda* of the *Kriya Yoga* Institute. He attended several *Kriya Yoga* retreats.

Publication List of H. P. Dhar

1. Molecular orientation in adsorption of pyridine and pyrazine at water/ mercury and water/air interfaces. B. E. Conway, H. P. Dhar, and S. Gottesfeld. *J. Colloid and Interface Science.* **43**(1975)303.
2. On adsorption isotherms for substitutional adsorption of molecules of different sizes. H. P. Dhar, B. E. Conway, and K. M. Joshi. *Electrochimica Acta.* **18**(1973)789.
3. Solvent structure and molecular orientation in the double layer at the mercury/water interface. B. E. Conway and H. P. Dhar. *Croatia Chemica Acta.* **45**(1973)109.
4. Solvent structure and molecular orientation behavior of adsorbed pyridine and pyrazine at the mercury/water interface. B. E. Conway, J. Mathieson, and H. P. Dhar. *J. Phys. Chem.* **78**(1974)1226.
5. Compensation effects in the thermodynamics of electrochemical adsorption of organic substances. B. E. Conway and H. P. Dhar. *Colloid and Polymer Science.* **253**(1975)11.
6. Hydration co-sphere and ion-pair interactions in electrochemical adsorption of organic N-cations. B. E. Conway and H. P. Dhar. *J. Colloid and Interface Science.* **48**(1974)73.
7. Adsorption behavior of 1,4-diazabicyclo octane at the mercury electrode. B. E. Conway and H. P. Dhar. *Electrochimica Acta.* **19**(1974)445.
8. On selection of standard states in adsorption isotherms. B. E. Conway and H. P. Dhar. *Electrochimica Acta.* **19**(1974)5.
9. Preliminary communication on molecular size factor and evaluation of interaction in terms in electrochemical isotherms. B. E. Conway and H. P. Dhar. *Surface Science.* **44**(1974)261.
10. On adsorption pseudo capacity. B. E. Conway and H. P. Dhar. *Discussion of Faraday Society.* **56**(1973).
11. Comparison of surface tension and electrochemical adsorption measurements from capillary electrometer and mercury drop-time

techniques. F. Kimmerle, H. Mennard, B. E. Conway, and H. P. Dhar. *Electrochimica Acta.* **19**(1974)883.

12. Gas-solid exchange reactions: Zinc vapor and polycrystalline zinc orthosilicate. E. A. Secco, H. P. Dhar, and Chien-Hou Su. *Can. J. Chemistry.* **42**(1974)3932.

13. Study of combined electroreflectance and double-layer effects on lead electrodes. H. P. Dhar. *Surface Science.* **66**(1977)449.

14. An electrochemical system for production of hydrogen and heavy water from off-peak electricity. S. Das Gupta, H. P. Dhar, J. Jacobs, and S. Mohanta. *Proc. Symp. on Industrial Water Electrolysis*, Vol 78-4, p. 282. Electrochemical Society Incorporated, Pennington, New Jersey.

15. Electrochemical inactivation of marine bacteria. H. P. Dhar, J. O'M. Bockris and D. H. Lewis. *J. Electrochem. Soc.* **128**(1981)229-231.

16. New trends in electrolytic reactor materials: Diaphragms. M. Islam, N. P. White, H. P. Dhar, and S. Das Gupta. *Polymer Plastic Technology Engineering.* **15**(1980)61-82.

17. Electrochemical diminution of surface bacterial concentration. H. P. Dhar, D. H. Lewis, and J. O'M. Bockris. *Can. J. Microbiol.* **27**(1981)998-1010.

18. A cathodic electrochemical method for microbial fouling prevention. H. P. Dhar, J. O'M. Bockris, and D. H. Lewis. *U.S. Patent No. 4.440,611.* 1984.

19. Use of in-situ electrochemical reduction of oxygen in diminution of adsorbed bacteria on metals in seawater. H. P. Dhar, D. W. Howell, and J. O'M. Bockris. *J. Electrochem. Soc.* **129**(1982)2178-2182.

20. Electrodeposition of cobalt tetraazaannulene dibromide on graphite electrodes. M. Yamana, R. Darby, H. P. Dhar, and R. E. White. *J. Electroanal. Chem.* **152**(1983)261-268.

21. The effect of heat treatment atmospheres on the electrocatalytic activity of cobalt tetraazaannulenes. H. P. Dhar, R. Darby, V. Y. Young, and R. E. White. *Electrochimica Acta.* **30**(1985)423-429.

22. Corrosion behavior of 70:30 Cu:Ni alloy in 0.5 M NaCl and in synthetic seawater. H. P. Dhar, R. E. White, R. Darby, R. B. Griffin, and G. Burnell. *Corrosion.* **41**(1985)193-196.

23. Corrosion of Cu and Cu:Ni alloys in 0.5 M NaCl and in synthetic seawater. H. P. Dhar, R. E. White, R. Darby, R. B. Griffin, G. Burnell, and L. R. Cornwell. *Corrosion.* **41**(1985)317-323.

24. Electrochemical methods for prevention of microbial fouling. *Modern Biochemistry.* Eds. H. Keyzer and F. Gutman. Plenum Press, New York, 1986. Chapter 22, pp. 593-606.

25. Performance study of a fuel cell Pt-on-Carbon anode in presence of CO and CO_2, and calculation of adsorption parameters of CO poisoning. H. P. Dhar, L. G. Christner, A. K. Kush, and H. C. Maru. *J. Electrochemical Society.* **133**(1986)1574.

26. On the effect of the Fe^{2+}/Fe^{3+} redox couple on oxidation of carbon in hot phosphoric acid. H. P. Dhar, L. G. Christner, and A. K. Kush. *J. Electroanal. Chem.* **213**(1986)161-167.

27. Modeling of CO poisoning of a fuel cell anode. H. P. Dhar, A. K. Kush, D. N. Patel, and L. G. Christner. *Electrochemical and Thermal Modeling of Batteries and Fuel Cells.* Eds. J. R. Selman and H. C. Maru. The ECS Softbound Proceeding Series, Princeton, N. J. 1986. pp. 284-297.

28. Nature of CO adsorption during hydrogen oxidation in relation to modeling for CO poisoning of a fuel cell anode. H. P. Dhar, L. G. Christner, and A. K. Kush. *J. Electrochem. Soc.* **134**(1987)3021-3026.

29. Corrosion of graphite composites in phosphoric acid fuel cells. L. G. Christner, H. P. Dhar, M. Farooque, and A. K. Kush. *Corrosion.* **43**(1987)571-575.

30. A new concept for high-cycle-life LEO: Rechargeable MnO_2-Hydrogen. A. J. Appleby, H. P. Dhar, Y. J. Kim, and O. J. Murphy. *J. Power Sources.* **29**(1990)333-340.

31. Utilization of dissolved oxygen in water in preventing microbial fouling on metals. H. P. Dhar. *Electrochemistry in Transition: 20th to 21st Century.* Plenum Press, New York, 1991.

32. On the effect of magnetic field on electrophoresis. H. P. Dhar, S. Nath, and D. H. Lewis. *Texas J. Science.* **43**(1991)334-336.

33. A unitized approach to solid polymer electrolyte fuel cell. H. P. Dhar. *J. Applied Electrochem.* **23**(1993)32-37.

34. On solid polymer fuel cells. H. P. Dhar. *J. Electroanal. Chemistry.* **357**(1993)237-250.

35. Near ambient, unhumidified solid polymer fuel cell. H. P. Dhar. *U.S. Patent No. 5,242,764* (1993).

36. Near ambient unhumidified solid polymer fuel cell. H. P. Dhar. *U.S. Patent No. 5,318,863.* 1994.

37. Recent progress in proton exchange membrane fuel cells. N. K. Anand, A. J. Appleby, and H. P. Dhar, et al. *Proceedings of the 10th Hydrogen Energy Conference.* Cocoa Beach, FL. June 20-24, 1994. Vol 3. 1669-1679.

38. Internally humidified proton exchange membrane fuel cell. *Proceedings of the 29th Intersociety Energy Conversion Engineering Conference.* Vol. 2, pp. 865-870. 1994.

39. Method for catalyzing a gas diffusion electrode. H. P. Dhar. *U.S. Patent No. 5,521,020. 1996.*

40. Internally humidified high performance proton exchange membrane fuel cell. *1994 Fuel Cell Seminar.* Pub. Courtesy Associates, Inc. Washington, D.C. pp. 85-88.

41. Flow facilitator for improving operation of a fuel cell. H. P. Dhar, K. A. Lewinski. U.S. Patent #5,935,725 (1999).

42. Simplified proton exchange membrane fuel cells for space and terrestrial applications. H. P. Dhar, K. A. Lewinski, and V. K. Tripathi. Proceedings of the Space Technology & Applications International Forum (STAIF). January 1998. Albuquerque, NM.

43. Medium-term stability testing of proton exchange membrane fuel cell stacks as independent power units. H. P. Dhar. *J. Power Sources,* 143(2005)185-190.

44. Measurements of fuel cell internal resistances for the detection of electrode flooding. H. P. Dhar and S. K. Chaudhuri. *J. Solid State Electrochemistry.* 13(7)(2009)999.

45. Detection and verification of electrode flooding in single cell studies. H. P. Dhar and S. K. Chaudhuri. *ECS Transactions,* Vol. 17 (2009).

References

1. Paramahamsa Prajnananada. *The Universe Within*. ISBN3-902038-03-9. 2000

2. Paramahamsa Yogananda. *God Talks with Arjuna—Bhagavad Gita*. ISBN 0-87612-030-0. 1996.

3. A. C. Bhakatibedananda Swami Prabhupada. *Bhagavad Gita—As It Is*. 1990.

4. Swami Chinmayananda. *My Prayers*. Central Chinmaya Trust Publisher.

5. Swami Venkatashanda. *Christ, Krishna and You*. ISBN 0-9612762-0-2. 1983.

6. Charles P. DiFazio.*From Where Did You Come?* Bhagavan Satya Baba. ISBN 81-207-1928x. 1997.

7. Marshall Govindon. *Babaji and the 18 Siddah Kriya Yoga Tradition*. ISBN 1-895383005. 1996.

8. Satyananda Giri. *Yogananda Sanga—As I Have Seen and Understand Him*. ISBN 3-902038-22-5. 2005

9. *Paramahamsa* Prajnanananda. *Lahiri Mahasaya*. ISBN 3-901665-226. 1999.

10. V. T. Neelakantan, S. A. Ramaiah and Babaji Nagaraj. *The Voice of Babaji*. ISBN 1-895-383-23-4. 2003.

11. Bruce McEwen & Elizabeth McEwen. *The End of Stress as We Know It*. ISBN 0-309-07640-4. 2004

12. Sudha Bathina. *Yoga Pathway to the Divine –The Teachings of Paramahamsa prajnanananda*. ISBN 3-901665-60-0. 2002.

13. Roy Eugene Davis. A *Master Guide to Meditation & Spiritual Growth*. ISBN 0-87707287-6. 2002.

14. Donald Schnell. *The Initiation*. ISBN 1-930722-06-0. 2002.
15. Pujan Roka. *Bhagavad Gita on Effective Leadership*. ISBN 13:978-0-595-67447-3.2006.
16. Paramahamsa Hariharananda. *Kriya Yoga –In the flow of Omniscience*. ISBN 978-3-902038-65-4. 2007.
17. Paramahamsa Hariharananda. *Kriya Yoga—The Scientific Process of Soul Culture and Essence of All Religions*. ISBN 3-902038-19-5. 1977.
18. Paramhamsa Prajnananda. Pramhamsa *Hariharananda—River of Compasson*. ISBN 3-901665-24-2. 1999.
19. Swami Sivananda Radha. *Kundalini Yoga for the West*. ISBN. 0-913454-38-7. 1993.
20. Mani Bhowmik. *Code Name God – The Spiritual Odyssey of Man of Science*. ISBN 0-8245-2281-8. 2005. The Crossroad Publishing Co.
21. Footprints of the Master – Memories Baba *Hariharananda*. ISBN 978-3-902038. 2007. Pp.354-359 by Haripada Dhar.
22. Paramahamsa Prajnandanda *Divine Blossoms—The Lineage of Kriya Yoga Masters*. 2007.
23. Dipak Chopra. *Seven Spiritual Laws of Success*. ISBN 1-878424-11-4. 1994.
24. Roy Eugene Davis. *The Self-Revealed Knowledge that Liberates the Spirit*. ISBN 0-87707275-2. 1997.
25. Paramahamsa Prajnanananda.*Life and Values*. ISBN 3-902038-09-8. 2001.
26. Roy Eugene Davis. *Living in God*. Living in God. ISBN 0-87707-276-0. 1997.
27. John O'M. Bockris. The *New Paradigm*. ISBN 0-9767444-06. 2004.
28. Swami Omkarananda. *Universal Religion*. ISBN 81-89064-19-3. 2007.
29. Aphorisms by Swami Omkarananda. *Get in Touch with the Divine Light in You*. ISBN 81-89064-01-0. 2004.
30. Roy Eugene Davis. *Guidelines to Inspired Living*. 2006.
31. Stephen Knapp. Stephen-Knapp.com.
32. Paramahamsa Yogananda. *The Law of Success-Using the Power of Spirit to Create Health, Prosperity, and Happiness*. ISBN 0-87612-150-4. 1980.